A MOROCCO ANTHOLOGY

A MOROCCO ANTHOLOGY

Travel Writing through the Centuries

Edited by
Martin Rose

The American University in Cairo Press
Cairo   New York

Copyright © 2018 by
The American University in Cairo Press
113 Sharia Kasr el Aini, Cairo, Egypt
420 Fifth Avenue, New York, NY 10018
www.aucpress.com

Exclusive distribution outside Egypt and North America by I.B.Tauris & Co Ltd.,
6 Salem Road, London, W2 4BU

Dar el Kutub No. 26189/16
ISBN 978 977 416 846 8

Dar el Kutub Cataloging-in-Publication Data

Rose, Martin
        A Morocco Anthology: Travel Writing through the Centuries / Martin
    Rose—Cairo: The American University in Cairo Press, 2018.
        p.   cm.
        ISBN: 978 977 416 846 8
        1. Morocco—Description and Travel
        916.4

1 2 3 4 5   22 21 20 19 18

Designed by Fatiha Bouzidi
Layout by Cherif Abdullah
Printed in the United States of America

Contents

Introduction

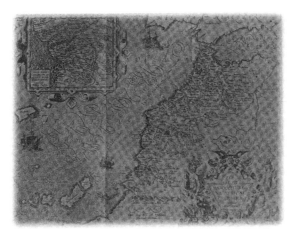

Morocco is not a country of one great city, like Istanbul, or Cairo, or Paris. It has four 'imperial cities,' where, in pre-colonial days, the sultan's peripatetic court settled for days, weeks, or months at a time on its constant travels around his

huge realm. The empire in its geographical heyday stretched from Tangier in the north to Timbuktu in the south, and the court, or makhzen, moved en masse around it to demand fealty and raise taxes. These imperial cities are Fes, Marrakech, Meknes, and what is today the capital, Rabat. Fes, with its near neighbor Meknes, was connected to Marrakech by a safe corridor of transit that ran through the Marmora Forest to Rabat, and on down the coast to Mogador and Marrakech. In addition, non-imperial Tangier stands on the Gibraltar strait, a Carthaginian settlement dominating the entrance to the Mediterranean, in turn a Portuguese, Spanish, and English colony and then in the twentieth century the internationally governed nerve-center of the foreign penetration into Morocco.

I have given each of these cities a chapter, and prefaced all with a short section on Morocco itself. For Morocco is a very different kind of country to most, defined across its long Islamic history not by hard borders but by the citing of the sultan's name at Friday prayers: the naming of the sultan proclaimed allegiance to him, and acknowledged his authority. Morocco had and perhaps still has memories of an almost metaphysical existence, with boundaries woven of sound and prayer; and a monarch who lived on the move and to this day has palaces in every city of the kingdom, each ready for use at a moment's notice. These cities had labile names, so that Marrakech was often known as Morocco City, a recognition of the kingdom's taking its own name from the 'southern' capital. Meknes was known to Europeans for much of its short history (it was raised as Louis XIV built Versailles) as Mequinez; Fes is often Fez, and the Portuguese cities and castles of the Atlantic coast rejoiced in wonderfully romantic names like Mogador, Mazagan, and Santa Cruz do Cabo de Gué, in which we can dimly make out Essaouira, al-Jadida, and Agadir.

This is a country like no other. For most Europeans it is the beginning of the non-European world. As the Catalan explorer and spy Ali Bey al-Abbasi wrote, arriving from Tarifa in Spain, in 1803, "The sensation which we experience on making this short passage for the first time can be compared only to the effect of a dream. Passing in so short an interval of time to a world absolutely new, and which has not the smallest resemblance to that which we have quitted, we seem to *have been actually transported into another planet." Morocco provides the visual vocabulary of Hollywood, with Moorish 'keyhole' arches defining Aladdin's Baghdad and every other film vision of the Arab Orient. It is astonishing how often our writers refer to 'the Arabian Nights,' which had nothing of course to do with Morocco at all. Today it is inevitably more familiar, but beneath the surface much remains of ways of thinking, and doing, that long predate Independence, the French Protectorate, and even Islam. Before 1912 Morocco was never part of any empire but its own. Its French and Spanish colonial period lasted only forty-four years, leaving a deep mark, to be sure, but not the profound psychological damage that French rule did to Algeria. It repays open-minded investigation and open-hearted enjoyment.*

The Empty Bled, 1920
Edith Wharton

Wharton writes lyrically of "a country so deeply conditioned by its miles and miles of uncitied wilderness that until one has known the wilderness one cannot understand the cities."

Between these nomad colonies lies the bled, the immense waste of fallow land and palmetto desert: an earth as void of life as the sky above it is of clouds. The scenery is always the same; but if one has the love of great emptinesses, and of the play of light on long stretches of parched earth and rock, the sameness is part of the enchantment. In such a scene every landmark takes on an extreme value. For miles one watches the little white dome of a saint's grave rising and disappearing with the undulations of the trail; at last one is abreast of it, and the solitary tomb, alone with its fig-tree and its broken kerb, puts a meaning into the waste. The same importance, but intensified, marks every human figure. The two white-draped riders passing single file up the red slope to that ring of tents on the ridge have a mysterious and inexplicable importance: one follows their progress with eyes that ache with conjecture . . . . vast distances unroll behind them, they breathe of Timbuctoo and the farthest desert. Just such figures must swarm in the Saharan cities, in the Soudan and Senegal. There is no break in the links; these wanderers have looked on at the building of cities that were dust when the Romans pushed their outposts across the Atlas.

Exhilarating Freedom, 1910
Ellis Ashmead-Bartlett

When the weather is fine and the roads in good condition, what can be more pleasant than a journey in the land of the Moors? The climate during the autumn and spring is perfect. The nights are cold, and you may find ice on the water in the early morning, but directly the sun appears the warmth is like that of a beautiful September day in England. The sky is never overcast by clouds, except when the rain is about to fall, and the atmosphere is one of a wonderful bluish transparency. I find something in the atmosphere of Morocco which I have not found in other countries,—something of freedom which is exhilarating to the mind and to the body. . . . There are none of the so-called conveniences and comforts of civilisation. There are no time-tables to be consulted, no arbitrary hours of departure and arrival, no right of road or speed limits to be observed. There are no bridges to the rivers, no taverns or rest-houses at which you can dine or stop for the night; no laws to be obeyed, and if there were, no authorities to carry them into effect. There is no one to protect you in case of danger, and you are entirely dependent on yourself for your food, your lodging, and safe-conduct.

Moroccan Hospitality, 1898
Robert Cunninghame Graham

After having drunk gallons of green tea, sat for an hour or two listening to stories of the Djinoun, smoked cigarettes and Kiff, and generally tried to imagine we were not disappointed, we retired to bed, so as before first light to be on the road. Our bedroom had no window and gave on the al fresco drawing-room; all around the walls were little recesses in which to put things, made in the thickness of the wall, pouches and powder horns hung from goats' horns forced underneath the thatch, three long "jezails" all hooped with silver—one with a Spanish two-real piece depending from the trigger-guard—stood in the corner, a lantern made of tin with coloured glass gave a red light, upon the floor of mud a Rabat carpet in pattern like a kaleidoscope or Joseph's coat was spread; nothing of European manufacture was there except a large-sized (navy pattern) Smith and Wesson pistol, which, hanging by a red worsted cord upon the wall, seemed to project the shadow of a cross upon the room.

Epicurean Missionaries, 1898
Robert Cunninghame Graham

Christians were rare, but missionaries not unknown. Their often self-indulgent habits were noted and enjoyed.

Almost all Europeans in Morocco must of necessity be merchants, if not they must be consuls, for there is hardly any other industry open to them to choose. The missionaries bought and sold nothing, they were not consuls; still they ate and drank, lived in good houses and though not rich, yet passed their lives in what the Jews called luxury. So they agreed to call them followers of Epicurus, for, as they said, "this Epicurus was a devil who did naught but eat and drink." The nickname stuck and changed into

"Bikouros" by the Moors, who thought it was a title of respect, became the name throughout Morocco for a missionary. One asks as naturally for the house of Epicurus on coming to a town as one asks for the "Chequers" or the "Bells" in rural England.

Fes

Fes, founded in 769 by Moulay Idris, is a city of extraordinary beauty. Paul Bowles, who knew it well, and whose novel The Spider's House *is one of its great evocations, describes it as "a vast, eternally spreading construction of cedar wood, marble, earth, and tiles, [which] has climbed up the sides and over the edge of the bowl" in which the city lies; and of Fes*

seen from the hills, "the vast oyster-grey Medina at their feet, formless honeycomb of cubes, terraces, courtyards, backed by the groved slopes of Djebel Zalagh." Titus Burckhardt, with even greater lyricism, called it "a geode of amethyst, brim-ful of thousands of tightly packed crystals, surrounded by a silver-green rim."

Premier, perhaps, among the imperial cities and the Maghreb's greatest seat of learning, Fes was also the first capi-tal of French Morocco, until its disorderly truculence encour-aged Maréchal Lyautey to relocate government to Rabat, which, being on the sea, was a great deal more accessible to the French navy. Fes is not the city that it was, of course, and it is a mistake to think of it as in any sense unchanged by colonial occupation or by the commercial onslaught of the nineteenth and twentieth centuries; but in Fes more than in any city of Morocco one can still catch glimpses, through half-closed eyes, of an older, more educated, more beautiful, and more arrogant city. There is much, too, left of the fabric, though the great palaces are mostly poor shadows of what they once were. Fes, a glorious anthill of a city that still pulsates, is mesmerizing and absorbing, a city of the imagination.

First Sight of Fes, 1616
William Lithgow

Many travelers attempted to describe the sensuous shock of first seeing Fes. Here is William Lithgow, described by one writer as "a hard, pugnacious, truculent Scot," arriving there in 1616.

The City of Fez is situate upon the bodies and twice double devalling faces of two hills, like to Grenada in Andelosia in Spain; the intervale, or low valley betweene both (through which the torride river of Marraheba runneth Southward) being the Center and chiefest place, is the most beautifull and populous part of the City; the situation of which, and of the whole, is just set under the Tropick of Cancer.

Over which River, and in this bottome, there are three score and seaven Bridges of stone and Timber, each of them being a passage for open streetes on both sides. The intervayle consisteth of two miles in length, and half a mile broad; wherein, besides five Cheareaffs or Market places, there are great Palaces, magnificke Mosquees, Colledges, Hospitals, and a hundred Palatiat Tavernes, . . . Most part of all which buildings, are three and foure stories high, adorned with large and open Windowes, long Galleries, spacious chambers, and flat tectures or square platformes.

The streetes being covered above, twixt these plaine-set Fabrickes, have large Lights cut through the tectur'd tops every where; in whose lower shoppes or Roomes are infinite Merchandize, and Ware of all sorts to bee sold.

The Women here go unmasked abroad, wearing on their heads, broad, and round Capes, made of Straw or small Reedes, to shade their faces from the Sunne; and damnable Libidinous . . . .

"The Chiefest Mosque," 1616
William Lithgow

Lithgow spent seventeen days at Fes, and made the most of his time there, unable (like most travelers of his age and not a few in our own) to resist the temptation of enumerating.

The two Hills on both sides the planur'd Citty, East and West, are over-cled with streetes and Houses of two stories high, being beautified also with delicate Gardens, and on their extreame devalling parts, with numbers of Mosquees and Watch-towers: On which heights, and round about the Towne, there stand some three hundred Wind-mils; most part whereof pertain to the Mosques, and the two magnifick Colledges erected for education of Children, in the Mahometanicall Law . . . .

The chiefest Mosque in it, is called Mammo-Currarad [al-Qarawiyin], signifying the glory of Mahomet, being an Italian mile in Compasse, and beautified with seventeene high ground Steeples, besides Turrets and Towers: having thirty foure entring Doores; being supported within, and by the length, with forty eight pillars, and some twenty three Ranges of pillars in breadth, besides many Iles, Quires and circulary Rotundoes: Every Pillar having a Lampe of Oyle burning thereat. . . . There are in the City besides it, more than foure hundred and threescore Mosquees; fifty whereof are well benefited and superbiously decored within and without, with glorious and extraordinary workmanship, whose rooffes within are all Mosaick worke, and curiously indented with Gold, and the walles and pillars being of grey Marble, inter-larded with white Alabaster.

This City aboundeth in all manner of provision fit for man or beast, & is the goodliest place of all North Affrick. . . . Truly, this is a World for a City.

Through a Sailor's Telescope, 1942
British Naval Intelligence Handbook

The NIH describes the city more briskly than Lithgow, in terms as useful to us today as to the beneficiaries of naval intelligence in 1942.

The tomb of Idriss II, the largest mosque in Morocco, and the ancient and famous university combine to make Fes the centre of Islam and its culture. The large native population, often lettered and wealthy, make it the most important political centre. Its many craftsmen, orga-nized in guilds, and its numerous traders make it also the principal native industrial and commercial centre of Morocco. Its industries range from carpet reed-mat making to silk embroidery and gilded-leather book-binding, and from leather-tanning and dyeing to pottery and native footwear. In its numerous and crowded bazaars almost anything from rich perfumes and spices to jewellery and silks, from native and imported wool and cotton fabrics and garments to copper and brass utensils, or from grain and dates to native sweetmeats and green tea are on sale. Long before the protectorate was established, its merchants maintained native representatives in London, Manchester and Lyons . . . .

Fes el Bali, the medina, is the home of a cultured aristocracy of rich merchants, of scholars and students, and of skilled craftsmen. Many of its houses are large and sumptuous, with splendid gardens. With its mosques, tombs, minarets and medersas, it is indeed a graceful, artistic and yet wealthy city. Much of Fes Djedid [New Fes], on the other hand, is inhabited by Saharan tribesmen, negroes, day-labourers, mokhzanis and men of the gish, living in small and crowded houses. . . . The French town, Ville Nouvelle, was begun in 1916 on previously agricultural land south-west of Fes Djedid. Since 1926 it has expanded considerably, and includes industrial, commercial and residential quarters, with modern hotels and tree-lined streets.

Fes from Above, 1889
Walter Harris

Walter Harris, the Times stringer and Correspondent from 1889 for more than two decades, who, despite his remarkable capacity for self-promotion and a somewhat fanciful imagination, was also at his best a fine descriptive writer, gives us this general description.

The views from all sides are lovely, one especially so, when one has reached the higher ground of the cemetery to the south of the town. On all sides are the domed tombs of the saints, while here and there a change in the scene is given by the dark green olive-trees. Far below one lies Fez, the whole city clearly visible. To the left is New Fez, with the Sultan's palace and park, and the many gardens with their white houses half-hidden in the trees; to the right lies Old Fez, one mass of flat roofs, in which scarcely a street can be traced, so narrow are they. Here, there, and everywhere rise the minarets of the many mosques. Between the cemetery and the town is a deep gully, through which flows one of the branches of the Wad Fas. High above the stream, on the summit of the steep bank, are the walls of the town, great stone and "tabbia" erections, of immense height, but fast falling to rack and ruin. Picturesque though in the extreme they are, half-covered with creepers, while on the old turreted towers have sprung up big trees and vines.

A Ruined Cambridge, 1889
Walter Harris

Fez is a charming old city. After all, it is only as if we let Cambridge fall a little more to ruin, give time to the statues on Caius gate to gain respectability by age, and to allow the grass to grow in full luxuriance over the John's and Trinity tennis courts. We would love Cambridge just the same then, I think; perhaps more. And I am sure I should prefer the wicked, idle city of Fez today to the bustling Fez of two or three centuries ago.

Football in Babouches, 1894
Stephen Bonsal

The *jeunesse dorée* of the Moroccan universities take their pleasures, apparently at least, very sadly. They never awaken the slumbering echoes of Fez with merry student songs. They have the stately deportment of Venetian notables, and many of them the girth of bishops. They have only one field sport, which they do not indulge in very frequently. It bears a ludicrous resemblance to football. They choose a field about a hundred yards long, and make narrow goals at each end. Then a wooden or a rope ball is thrown in their midst, which they kick about most dexterously. How they succeed in doing it without kicking off their *baboshas* or slippers is a mystery.

The Cordobans of Fez, 1910
Ellis Ashmead-Bartlett

From the very beginning there had been waves of immigrants to Fes, an early generation of exiles arriving from Cordoba in al-Andalus. They were settled in the Andalusian quarter of the city, which was constructed for them—and were assumed to give the city its fiercely pious and generally intolerant atmosphere.

The Moors of Fez are the descendants of the theologians who were expelled from Cordoba during the reign of the Sultan Hakam, after the great revolt in the year 808. They disliked the gay and sociable life led by Hakam and desired a return to the strict paths of Mohammedan asceticism. . . . Their rebellion failed, and they were bundled out of Andalusia across the Straits into Morocco. The first Moulai Edriss had just commenced to build Fez, and he was pleased to find a quarter in his new city for the eight thousand refugees who had fled from Cordoba. The theologians expelled from Cordoba have transmitted the same characteristics to their descendants, and down through thirteen centuries the strict observance of their religion has been the dominating factor of life at the capital. The people of Fez are still, as they were in the days of Hakam, the most bigoted and fanatical of all the tribes and races who embrace the Mohammedan religion, . . . nowhere is the Infidel more disliked and his presence more resented, than at Fez. . . . It is said that some of the old families of Fez still guard the keys of their old homes in Cordoba, which they carried away when expelled for their ill-timed rebellion. The rust and decay of thirteen centuries have probably long since disposed of the keys of the houses of Cordoba, but the tradition of a return to the warm sunshine, blue skies and well-watered plains of Andalusia still survives amongst the citizens of Fez.

Morocco Bound—Cordovan Leather, 1901
Budgett Meakin

It is said that Cordovan refugees introduced the art of dyeing and preparing the famous Cordovan—now known as Morocco—leather, from the name of which is derived our word cordwainer, as also the French cordon-nier, an evidence of the early popularity of this article.

The Fez and the Handkerchief, 1860
James Richardson

In a curious non-sequitur, which none the less tells us about the eponymous headwear, Richardson notes that:

Fez, indeed, could make no bona-fide resistance to a European army. The chief manufactures are principally woollen hats, silk handkerchiefs, slippers and shoes of excellent leather, and red caps of felt, commonly called the fez; the first fabrication of these caps appears to have been in this city.

Andalusian Roots of Fasi Culture, 1898
Robert Cunninghame Graham

The constant circulation of people and culture between Muslim Spain and North Africa continued until the expulsion of the last Moriscos from Spain in 1614.

Fez has the mixture of Spanish blood in its inhabitants which the expulsed from Malaga, Granada, and from all the Andalos, brought and disseminated. In the high houses, which make the streets like sewers to walk in, you hear men play the lute, and women sing the Malagueña, Caña and the Rondeña as in mountain towns in Spain. Quite half the population have fair hair, some pale blue eyes, and their fanaticism is born of ancient persecution by the fanatic Christians of Spain. In every house, in every mosque, in almost every saint's tomb, is fine tile-work, stone and wood-carving, the eaves especially being often as richly decorated as they had been Venetian and not African. The streets are thronged, men move quickly through them, and the whole place is redolent of aristocracy, of a great religious class, in fact has all the air of what in Europe we call a capital.

The Narrow, Dark Streets of Fes, 1901
Budgett Meakin

Most of the streets of Fez are exceedingly narrow, and as the houses are higher than is usual in this country, besides being often built over the thoroughfares, these are gloomy and dark, an effect which is heightened in summer by training vines or stretching awnings across the busier avenues—some of which indeed are permanently roofed with wood. From this in part results the pallor for which their inhabitants are noted, considered a mark of distinction and therefore jealously guarded. Many of the houses have to be supported by props and stays across the streets, but there is less of that half-ruined, half-decayed appearance, so typical of eastern towns. One cause of this difference lies in the fact that the materials employed in building are wooden beams, rough stones, tiles and mortar, in lieu of the tabiah, or mud-concrete, which is attended by much outward crumbling.

Outside and Inside a Moroccan Palace, 1890
Pierre Loti

The French traveler Pierre Loti describes with delight the house and its gardens in which he was accommodated. As is generally the case in Fes, and in many other Arab cities, the exterior gave little clue to the luxury within.

So narrow was the street that we had some difficulty dismounting. But there was no time to lose. On getting out of the saddle we had to throw ourselves straight into the small, low old door and go straight in, to avoid being crushed by the horseman behind who arrived immediately after us, himself pushed onwards by all the others in the column. I fell virtually onto the bayonets in a guardpost full of soldiers commanded by a sort of ancient black janissary, who was under orders not to let any of these new French guests go out without an armed escort.

These first impressions were hardly pleasing; but in Morocco one must not worry about the outside of houses; the most miserable entrances lead often to enchanted palaces.

Once past the gate we arrived in a delicious garden: great orange trees, white with flowers, were planted in serried ranks above a tangle of roses, jasmines, citronellas and wallflowers. From here a paved avenue led us to another door, very low too, at the foot of a high wall. This gave onto a court like the Alhambra, its arcades scalloped, in arabesques and mosaics, with water gushing into the marble basins. . . . It is here that the ambassador must undergo, at the beginning, the three days of quarantine and purification that is obligatory for all foreigners who have the privilege of entering Fez.

The Human Beehive, 1910
Ellis Ashmead-Bartlett

The greatest religious institution in Fes was the tomb of Moulay Idris, forbidden—like all Moroccan mosques—to unbelievers. Ashmead-Bartlett describes the religious galaxy of which Moulay Idris was the greatest star, and the medina in which it was set.

The most sacred shrine is the mosque of Moulai Edriss, where the founder of the city lies buried. Moulai Edriss is the founder and patron saint of the capital. Everything is done in his name, and all the ceremonies—such as births, marriages and circumcisions—are celebrated at the mosque which bears his name. Riding through the streets the air resounds with cries of "Moulai Edriss!"

"Moulai Edriss!" for the countless beggars and cripples call blessings on your head in his name. The two largest and most famous mosques in Fes bear the titles of the two quarters into which Fes Bali was divided on its foundation, namely, El Kairaouiynin and Andalous, and both were built in the year 859 by the sons of a rich widow who came to settle in the town. The former is so large that no less than 22,000 people can pray in it at the same time. It formerly possessed a library, taken from the King of Seville at the conquest of that province in 1285, but unfortunately the majority of the books and manuscripts have been lost in the succeeding centuries as it was the improvident custom of the teachers who gave lessons in the mosque to allow the students to carry away the books with them. . . .

The only simile which will give a correct impression of the Medina during the busy hours of the day is to imagine a human beehive, with each bee sitting cross-legged in its own little cell, with thousands of others passing to and from gathering their honey—the necessities of everyday life. These little booths are all of a size, namely, about six feet wide, six feet running back from the road, and four to five feet in height. In them you may find as many as half a dozen toilers, sitting cross-legged on the floor, each engaged in his particular trade. The variety of occupations is infinite: metal-workers, silk vendors, grocers, pottery sellers, charcoal-burners, leather-workers, fancy goods sellers, clothes outfitters, bootmakers, butchers, are all found in these same little booths, pleased to sell the smallest quantity of any article to the humblest of purchasers. But the marked feature of Fez is the astonishing number of its fruit shops, and it is no exaggeration to say that every other shop contains fruit and vegetables. The citizens of the capital rely largely on fruit during the hot weather, and they are supplied from their numerous gardens, and by the surrounding tribes, who do a good business with the capital. The principal fruit and vegetables are potatoes, very fine tomatoes, marrows, cucumbers, figs, water-melons.

Dangers to Christians, 1910
Ellis Ashmead-Bartlett

The Fasis, civilised and cultured though they be, have not borrowed any of the second-hand attractions of Europe like the Japanese. Their customs and their culture are peculiarly their own, and have thrived for centuries, a bright torch in the Sais valley, whilst Europe was still plunged in the darkness and ignorance of the Middle Ages. . . . Its citizens are the most fanatical of all Mohammedans, and the execration in which Christians are held has been deepened by the aggressive action of France. . . . But the religious Moor is just, even when blinded by dislike of the Nazarene, and he has divided the Christians of the world into two classes, namely, those who are French and those who are not. . . .

The very air of the town breathes serious devotion. Every street has its mosque, and every mosque its devout worshippers at all hours of the day. No Christian dare enter, or even glance for that matter, within those sacred portals, for his life in the present state of public opinion, would most assuredly pay the forfeit. It is best to hurry past the mosques with your head turned the other way, and to pretend to ignore, or not to understand, the muttered curses and pious throat-clearing which follow your polluted passage.

The Tomb of Moulay Idris, 1901
Budgett Meakin

The streets which approach its entrance are sacred, and are an inviolable sanctuary, being considered in this respect equal to a mosque, so that Jews, Christians and four-footed beasts are not allowed within, though it is not necessary to remove one's slippers. The ends of the streets have chains or bars across to mark them, and they are very well paved with red bricks. The principal one, which runs up to the Tuniat door of the saint's tomb, has a pretty arched gate. (I was very near trouble in this street one day, when my eye-glasses having aroused suspicion, I was hailed by a shop-keeper with a summons to testify to Mohammed, but removing them, I affected not to hear, and before the lethargic zealot could leave his shop, I was well round the corner, lost into the crowd, as I was clad like a native.) In this one the shops are of a better class, and sell special articles. Among them are native bees' wax candles to burn round the tomb, for those of foreign manufacture would not be holy enough. . . .

Gold-braided hangings adorn the walls [of the shrine], and carpets—both native and European—the floors. Exquisitely carved and painted Arabesques give warmth to the ceiling, from which are suspended lanterns and chandeliers in profusion, one of the former being of great size—eight feet high it is said. These are interspersed with numerous oil-lamps—tumblers with floating wicks—while several handsome candle-sticks stand on the floor so that there is no lack of glare, and the heat when the place is crowded must be intense, especially when it is remembered how many of the worshippers bring candles. Among other conspicuous ornaments, after the native fashion, are two large 'grand-father' clocks, and three round gilt time-pieces. . . . The natives believe that the angel Gabriel periodically visits the shrine, and that if any worshipper has the good luck to touch the hem of his garment, his entry to Paradise is secured. The chance of such a fortunate event is enough in itself to attract these con-science-stricken sinners, and doubtless accounts in some measure for the crowds who daily pay their respects there.

The University and 'Learned Ignorance,' 1901
Budgett Meakin

Fes was a city with a great university in the Qairouiyyine, and the remnants at least of extraordinary libraries.

Of colleges the only remains are seven madarsahs, con-taining chambers which accommodate among them per-haps one thousand five hundred students who 'read' at the Karûeeïn. They pay no rent, but buy the keys of the rooms from the last occupant, selling them again on leav-ing. At the mosque they are taught by 'ulamà or 'wise men' who are supported from property of which part has been bequeathed for the special endowment of 'chairs,' the same expression being used in Morocco as in Europe. . . . Fes has a reputation for learning, and undoubtedly the wisest men in the Empire are to be found here, but by reason of their pride and bigotry the best of them deserve the title someone bestowed upon them of 'ignorant learned.' Their sultans have ever found the Fasis difficult to manage, especially on account of the large number of hereditary saints who so easily rouse their fellow-citizens. It is a noteworthy fact that Fes is at once the most religious and the most wicked city of Morocco, according to the Moors' own reckoning, the saints and sinners being for the most part identical. . . .

The present tower was built with a fifth of the booty taken from foreigners. On the top was placed a ball covered with gold and encrusted with precious stones, surmounted by the sword of Idrees II, whose descendants quarrelled with the builders, and in vain attempted to recover it. This tower having become the abode of storks and pigeons, it was repaired in 1289. . . . On a dome built where the original tower had stood, were laced talismans on iron spikes, to shield the place from evil, such as a bird holding a scorpion in its beak, to prevent the entrance of those insects; a ball to frighten serpents away; and one to keep mice out. Most remarkable stories

are told to prove the efficacy of these not very Mohammedan devices.

Libraries in Decay, 1889
Walter Harris

There still remain in Fez some relics of the great libraries
that in former times were the chief ornament of the place,
but the books have been worm-eaten almost to dust, and
decay and damp have set their indelible seal upon the
manuscripts. Nevertheless there must still be works of
great value hidden away in the recesses of the library that
adjoins the Kairouin mosque, which probably will never
come to light till some European power takes possession
of the country. I am thankful I shall not be a schoolboy in
that day, for rumour says that the lost books of Euclid—
are there such things as lost books of Euclid?—lie hidden
there, with some of Livy's undiscovered works.

The Shops of Fes, 1889
Walter Harris

Fas Bali, or Old Fez, is the commercial part of the town
. . . and contains the Fondaks and shops. The streets here
are narrower than in New Fez, but far more picturesque,
for instead of the tall garden walls on either hand there
are the little box-like shops, full of rich colouring and
dirt, smells of incense and dead cats and containing also
the shop-owner, who sits cross-legged, counting his beads
perhaps, and scarcely paying any attention to his business
or the rare sight of Christians.

One long street, roofed in from the sun, forms the
highway of Fez. It runs from New Fez, right through the
town, ending opposite one of the many gates of the Kairouin mosque. In this street are exposed for sale almost
every article one can imagine, but curiously enough
the shops that contain only one variety of goods are all
together, for instance there are a dozen shops full of old
iron or metal, old brass and copper kettles, bolts, chains
and screws; the next cluster contains old daggers, swords
and knives, while a little further on is a district of shoe

shops. Others again are full of Manchester goods, linens and calicoes, cretonnes and beads, and many an item besides, while a whole street is given up to pottery. These shops are for the most part only some few feet square, so that there is not room for a large stock. The floor of the shop is elevated some few feet above the level of the street, and boarded over; on the boards is a carpet, and on the carpet, the shop-owner. The front of the shop is a shutter that opens upwards. A piece of rope is used by the shop-man to scramble in by.

Shopping for the Sharifa, 1912
Emily Keene

Emily Keene, the English widow of the Sharif of Ouazzane, was too distinguished to do her own shopping. On her visit to the Sultan in Fes after the death of her husband, in 1892, she was besieged in her lodgings by merchants specialising in all the luxuries that Fes could offer.

Once I was installed [at my house in Fes] deputations

came daily, most fatiguing on account of the torrid heat. Then I had to see jewellers to order ear-rings, large hooped ones of gold with five pendants, each ornamented with coral beads; such a weight, I should imagine, for the ears. I also ordered a pearl necklace of fifteen strands. These are bought by weight, and arranged with no idea of regularity of size, though the colour is taken into consideration. As a mass, the necklace is most effective, especially when supplemented by another to outline it in gold, almost like a lot of fishes, which hang on small pieces of fantastic designs, or the contrasting necklace a black one interspersed with seed-pearls. The black necklace is made of a composition of amber, musk and many other sweet-scented ingredients, mixed into a paste and exposed to the sun to dry and harden. When well made with the best ingredients, the perfume lasts for years. I had next to choose gold bracelets and anklets and several rings, all of native manufacture. Then I had to see brocaded silks, silk haiks, the enormous belt of gold thread and variegated silk embroidered thereon, velvet slippers embroidered in gold thread, coloured leather ones, a crimson scarf with threads of gold, another called the cloth of gold, and the veil, which is really more like a scarf, of raw silk woven in cross-bar fashion.

The Waters of Fes, 1613
Samuel Purchas

Writers on Fes all commented on its waters.

So doth the River disperse itselfe into manifold Channels; no sooner entring the Citie but it is divided, as it were, into many Fingers, in varietie of Water Courses, insinuating itselfe into every Street and Member thereof: and not contented thus in Publike to testifie Affection, finds means of secret Intelligence with his love by Conduit Pipes . . . which still enjoying, he wooeth, and ever wooing, enjoyeth.

Washing the Streets, 1901
Budgett Meakin

They often noted, too, the sanitary practice of periodically flushing out the streets with running water.

In almost every street may be heard the sound of running streams, and often the splashing and grinding of mills is added to the varied sounds with which the air is filled. Under the houses and through them, its volume swelled by the water from springs in the town, and by conduits bringing special supplies for special people, the river rolls along, and though it affords an excellent means of flushing the drains—which on this account are by no means so odoriferous as those in the other towns—it creates an unhealthy dampness, as the countenances of the citizens betoken.

When the town becomes very dirty and muddy the water is allowed to run down the streets by opening lids for the purpose in the conduits, and stopping the ordinary flows of the water, so that it overflows and cleanses the paving, to the inconvenience of shod, and the delight of unshod, passers-by.

Demons of the Bath-house, 1816
Ali Bey al-Abbassi

Fez contains a great number of public baths. Some of them are good and contain different rooms, which are heated to different temperatures; so that you may always chuse that which suits you best. In all these rooms you find large basons into which hot water is continually coming from the boilers placed behind, and also numerous stone bottles, which serve either for bathing or for making the necessary legal ablutions. I have already observed, that on entering these rooms, all the body is covered with a subtle dew, because the atmosphere is completely saturated with the vapour of the hot water. . . .

All the rooms are vaulted and without windows; they have only small holes in the roof to receive the daylight, which are filled with glass. The floor is chequered with well arranged various colours. . . .

The men go there in the morning, and the women in the evening. I went there generally at night and took the whole house to myself, in order to prevent interruption from strangers . . . The first time I went there I observed that pails full of hot water were placed with symmetry in the corners of every room and cabinet. I asked the reason of this? "Do not touch them, sir," answered all the people belonging to the bath; "do not touch them!" Why not? "These pails are for the people below." Who are they? "The demons who come here to bathe themselves at night." On this topic they told me many ridiculous stories. As I have this long while declared war against the devil and all his earthly vicegerents, I had the satisfaction of employing in my bath some of these pails of water, and of thus depriving the poor devils of their entertainment.

Economics of the Slave Market, 1901
Budgett Meakin

Other features of the city that attracted regular comment were the slave-market and the Jewish quarter—the mellah.

Meakin comments on the slave-market as he might have on a grain-market, quite unsentimentally.

The slave-market is held every afternoon at ten minutes before sunset, in an enclosure used in the early morning for the sale of wool, and afterwards for that of grain. When caravans from the Sahara come in, slaves are plentiful, but like most other articles of commerce, they become scarce and dear in the wet season, when sales are effected privately through the auctioneers.

The Jewish Quarter, 1901
Budgett Meakin

The mellah, or Jewish quarter, forms one of the noticeable features of New Fez, . . . which constitutes the largest Jewish colony in the Empire. . . . The Jews go about with white-spotted blue handkerchiefs over their heads, and the Jewesses affect big red ones with white patterns, four of which, woven in one piece, are worn over the head and folded in front, much as the Moorish women wear their haiks. Their indoor dress requires a chapter to itself, but its most noteworthy local features are a high peaked head-dress or silken kerchief, starched cone-shape, and an unusually low and scanty bodice. As in the other inland towns, with a few exceptions the Jews are not allowed to go shod or to ride outside their quarter, and they may not ride horses at all. Except in the business centre, and in the portions immediately adjacent to the mellah, the number of Jews to be encountered is very small,—especially in bad weather—which is not surprising in view of the restrictions and indignities imposed upon them.

The Mythology of Storks, 1816
Ali Bey al-Abbassi

Ali Bey notes the hospital, but is rapidly side-tracked onto the fascinating business of storks—a constant feature of the Moroccan landscape then, as now.

Fez has an hospital which is very richly endowed, and used only for the treatment of lunatics. It is very strange that a great part of the funds to maintain this establishment have been bequeathed by the wills of various charitable testators with the express purpose of assisting and nursing sick cranes and storks, and of burying them when dead.

They believe that the storks are men from some distant islands, who at certain seasons of the year take the shape of birds to come here; that they return again at a certain time to their country, where they resume their human form till the next season.

For this reason it would be considered a crime to kill one of these birds. They tell thousands of ridiculous stories upon this occasion. Undoubtedly, it is the utility of these animals, who are continually making war with the reptiles which abound so much in hot climates, which has occasioned the general respect and anxiety for their preservation. But the love of the marvellous, here as elsewhere, has substituted absurd fables for the actual truth.

Amulets for Sickness, 1912
Emily Keene

Medicine was very much a preoccupation, and western trav-
elers were generally supposed to be expert. Cunninghame
Graham traveled disguised as a doctor; William Lemprière
was one; and Emily Keene, though the widow of perhaps the
greatest hereditary saint in the empire, was also expected to
perform miracles (a particular blend of medical knowledge
and baraka) in the harem of the Basha of Fes.

The ladies were most gorgeously dressed and weighed
down with jewels. Some had a form of head-dress that
made them look as though they had horns, and when
they stood up one almost thought the weight must throw
them on their backs. Their gait under this load was not
graceful, as you saw they must adjust their bodies to sup-
port this extraordinary adornment to the head. The Basha
took it for granted that I must have a knowledge of medicine, and explained his troubles almost too minutely. His
eyes were in a state of chronic ophthalmia; granulation

was thick, and I told him I would give him an eye-wash to reduce the inflammation. The ladies' conversation related principally to their ailments, and particularly requested amulets, written for them then and there by Muley Ali.

Powder-play and Horsemanship, 1889
Walter Harris

Any traveler in Morocco would be unlucky not to see what is today often called a fantasiya, *a display of masculinity, horsemanship and skill with a gun that was even more exciting when Harris saw it than it is today.*

We stopped to see the troops at their Lab-al-Baroud or powder play. From a dozen to twenty men would stand in line of horseback at the end of an open piece of ground; at a given signal they would urge their horses to a canter, salute with their long guns, waving them round their turbaned heads, change from a canter to a furious gallop, and crying out "Allah! Allah!" fire. Nothing could surpass the picturesqueness of the tearing horses, the riders' flowing garments borne in the wind behind them, the gorgeous trappings of the horses, the men's ease and grace in the saddle. Over and over again they repeated it, till one's head was almost turned with the brilliant sight and the quick volleying.

The Culinary Preparation of Hashish, 1816
Ali Bey al-Abbassi

One of the entertainments enjoyed at Fes, the product of the mountains of the Rif, was hashish, or as it is called in Morocco, kif. Ali Bey, amateur anthropologist that he was, gives us an account of its elaborate preparation.

This country provides in abundance a kind of narcotic plant called kiff; as it grows only in spring, I have not seen it in blossom, but only dried, and almost reduced to powder. In order to make use of it, they boil it with a good deal of butter in an earthen pot for twelve hours together; they afterwards strain the butter and it serves to seasons their victuals; or they mix it with sweetmeats, or swallow it in the form of pills. It is said, that in whatever form it is taken, its effect is very certain: others smoke the leaves of the plant instead of tobacco. I have been told that its merit is, that it does not intoxicate, but raises the spirits, and fills the imagination with agreeable fancies.

The Sultan and his Umbrella, 1816
Ali Bey al-Abbassi

Many travelers to Fes describe the sultan and being received by him, generally over-egging the pudding. Here is Ali Bey, at the beginning of the nineteenth century, giving us the pageantry, as well as a pointed glimpse of his own importance as he calls on Moulay Sulaiman.

The retinue of the Sultan was composed of a troop of fifteen to twenty men on horseback; about an hundred steps behind them came the Sultan, who was mounted on a mule, with an officer bearing his umbrella, who rode by his side, also on a mule. The umbrella is a distinguishing sign of the Sovereign of Morocco. Nobody but himself, his sons, and his brothers, dare to make use of it; however I had this high honour conferred on me. Eight or ten servants walked by his side, the minister Salaoui followed him on a mule with a servant walking. The retinue was closed by some officers and about a thousand of white and black soldiers on horseback, with long guns in their hands, and forming a sort of line of battle whose centre was composed of ten or twelve men, and whose extremities ended in a point of only one man; but neither rank, file, or distance was observed. The centre of the line had a front of thirteen large standards.

A Royal Railway, 1905
Gabriel Veyre

From the last days of independent Morocco come many tales of the Sultans both at Fes and Marrakech. These accounts often make fun of these rulers, no doubt exaggerating the naivety with which they embraced the more trivial technologies of the West. But there was a dangerous cocktail of extravagance and credulousness which allowed unscrupulous Europeans to make a great deal of money. Here is Gabriel Veyre, the Sultan Abdel Aziz's French photography teacher, on the subject of railways.

Abdel Aziz wanted a railway. Oh! A small railway, a poor little local railway with a straight track, which allowed him to travel from his palace to his gardens at Dar-Dbi-bar four kilometers away. 'Decauville' track was ordered from Creusot, a pretty little locomotive and two darling saloon cars, richly upholstered, dolled up to the nines and altogether exquisite. The news arrived that everything was ready, packed up, despatched—and then that it been landed at Larache. You can scarcely imagine what went into transporting packages like these from the coast to Fez. Loaded onto wagons to each of which were hitched sixty mules, the wagons, the locomotive and the rails took four long months to reach us on 150 kilometers of track across the desert. A less patient man than Abdel Aziz would have lost his head over it.

The moment the packing-cases were opened, the installation of the track and the assembly of the rolling-stock began. But owing to terribly bad luck, no one ever succeeded in finding the engine's wheels. Searches were made at Larache, demands made of the customs, the shipping company, the French railways and at Creusot. But no wheels ever arrived.

While waiting, the Sultan decided that the train would

be pulled by mules, or horses. He wanted no delays, and scarcely two kilometers of track were in place when he gave himself the pleasure of making an expedition. After which, quite satisfied, he forgot about his railway. Today the rails are buried deep, and no one gives them a thought.

Marrakech

Probably for today's visitors the most famous city of Morocco, Marrakech has become something of a tourist-magnet, over-endowed with identikit hotels and noisy bus-parties. But it has an odd capacity to absorb tourists, and outside the

Djamaa el-Fna and the main sights, one can still vanish comfortably enough into the lanes and alleys of what the tourist authorities refer to as 'the Ochre City.' It seems to be in great disrepair—but probably always did—and the sights that strike the eye with such unforgettable pleasure, the Atlas mountains capped with snow, the Koutoubia tower in the foreground, the Fna at night, perhaps seen from the terrace of the Café de France, are almost as memorable today as they ever were (almost, because the Fna above all has been domesticated, its fires damped, its cooks brigaded into brightly lit booths, its charlatans tamed). Palm trees sighing gently in the evening breeze above the pink plaster walls built of what travelers called 'tabby,' great gardens, the breathtaking open space of the Badi', the palace of the Saadian Sultans, all these remain, along with the warren of the suqs and the confusing maze of gates and walls.

'Morocco City' was the southern capital of the Sultans, where they held court facing the Sahara. Into Marrakech marched the army of the eunuch Pasha Jawdar fresh from the conquest of Timbuktu in 1591, with his English cannon and European musketeers. From Marrakech set out the great

armed progresses that kept the lands beyond the High Atlas intermittently in thrall and even paying taxes. Here in the slave-markets and suqs the wealth of sub-Saharan Africa, ivory, gold, peacock feathers, was traded, a flow of wealth that gave Sultan Ahmed al-Mansour the epithet of al-Dhahabi, the 'Golden One.' Its heyday, though, was fairly short and an English merchant called John Smith in the early seventeenth century noted that Marrakech "for the most part, is defaced, but by the many pinnacles and towers with balls on their tops, hath much appearance of much sumptuousnesse and curiositie . . . the houses in most parts lye tumbled one above another, the walls of earth are with the great fresh flouds washed to the ground . . . most only reliques of lamentable ruines and sad desolation."

Here much of the patronizing and jaundiced contact took place between canny foreigners and the later Alaouite Sultans, who were charmed, conned, and bullied into submission. The process of subjugation was all too familiar: "By 1902," writes Gavin Maxwell in his incomparable Lords of the Atlas, *"the imperial coffers of Morocco had been drained to the last dregs to pay for the Sultan's toys and the multiple commissions on them that amounted to almost five hundred per cent. As a result the Viziers had obtained gigantic loans from European powers, loans that precluded possibility of any independent Morocco in the future."*

First Sight of Marrakech with the High Atlas, 1898
Robert Cunninghame Graham

Above the forests of tall date palms which fringe the town, the tall mosque towers rose, the Kutubieh and the minaret of Sidi Bel Abbas high above the rest. From the green gardens of the Aguedal the enormous stone-built pile of the Sultan's palace, all ornamented with fine marbles brought from Italy and Spain, towered like a desert-built Gibraltar over the level plain. Across the sea-like surface of the steppe long trains of camels, mules and men on foot crawled, looking like streams of ants converging on a giant ant-hill, whilst in the distance the huge, wall-like Atlas towering up, walled the flat country in, as the volcanoes seem to cut off Mexico from the world outside.

Nothing to Recommend It but Its Great Extent, 1793
William Lemprière

Lemprière, a century earlier, was a little less star-struck by the city itself.

The city of Morocco . . . is situated in a beautiful valley, formed by a chain of mountains on the Northern side, and those of the Atlas, from which it is distant about twenty miles on the South and East. The country which immediately surrounds it is a fertile plain, beautifully diversified with clumps of palm trees and shrubs, and watered by small and numerous streams, which descend from Mount Atlas. The Emperor's out-gardens, which are situated at the distance of about five miles to the South of the city, and are large plantations of olives walled in, add considerably to the beauty of the scene.

Morocco, though one of the capitals of the empire— for there are three, Morocco, Mequinez and Fez—has nothing to recommend it but its great extent, and the royal palace. It is enclosed by remarkably strong walls, built of tabby, the circumference of which is about eight miles.

The Navy in Descriptive Mode, 1942
British Naval Intelligence Handbook

Less romantic, naturally, but always useful (perhaps particularly in revising Lemprière's optimistic estimate of the distance from the Atlas), is the Naval Intelligence Handbook of 1942.

Marrakech, the southern capital and the largest native city of Morocco, is about 40 miles from the foothills of the High Atlas and 2½ miles south of the left bank of Oued Tensift, at an altitude of 1,475 feet. . . . It is the principal commercial city and resort for the tribesmen of the High Atlas and much of the north-west Sahara. It spreads widely over the vast well-irrigated plain of the Haouz, and with its straight streets and gigantic city wall it has some of the characteristic features of a Sudanese town. It is surrounded by vast date-palm groves, with orchards of olive, orange and other fruit-trees as well as vineyards. The Koutoubia mosque minaret is a landmark visible for many miles across the plain.

The Vortex of Djamaa el-Fna, 1932
Wyndham Lewis

Marrakech is indeed "the mouth of the Sahara" . . . . It is a huge, red, windy metropolis of mud and sand. In the centre of it is "The Place of Destruction" (*Djemaa el Fna*) which is a small desert in the midst of a city, full of vigorous African crowds—acrobats, potters, Chleuh boy-dancers (like bands of depraved but still strictly disciplined surpliced acolytes)—many sorcerers and palmists (before whom squats some silent mountaineer, drinking in the words of fate, while the prophetic quack holds fast the tell-tale hand, mesmerising his victim as he whispers to him the secrets of the future) with, at the busy hours, a city of fantastic tents. The tent-making capacities of the natural nomad are here seen to full advantage, in the structures of mats and poles, which take the shapes of a pachydermatous beast, or hollow carnival giant, sheltering the salesman and artisan—cobblers, locksmiths, couscous vendors, herbalists, butchers, letter-writers.

The Razing of the Badi' Palace, 1889
Walter Harris

On the fragile, transient beauty of the city, and the vindictive, almost Mesopotamian possession-by-destruction with which one dynasty took over from the last, Harris is unusually poetic.

Of the palaces of former dynasties nothing but the merest ruins remains—a few walls at Fez of the palace of the Merinides, and at Marrakesh the great walls and enclosure of what must once have been the finest of all Moroccan buildings, the palace of the Saadien Sultans, whose dynasty came to an end in the seventeenth century. Their mausoleum, dating from the sixteenth century, the most beautiful building in Morocco, still remains intact as an example of perfect Moorish art; and there is no doubt, from contemporary descriptions, that the neighbouring palace was of unparalleled beauty and magnificence. The ground-plan of its great courtyard, with its immense water-tanks and its fountains, can still be clearly traced; while at one end, facing a long, straight tiled walk between two of the great basins, are the ruins of the Sultan's audience-chamber, a vast, square room. The walls are still standing, but the roof has fallen long ago. The description of this palace in the days of its glory reads like a page from the Thousand and One Nights. What had taken a century to build was destroyed in a day. The Saadien dynasty fell, and the cruel despot, Mulai Ismail, seized the throne. His first act was to order the destruction of this famous palace of his predecessors, and the great building was looted by the soldiery and the crowd. Many of the old houses in Marrakesh today have doorsteps formed of small columns, or parts of larger ones, of rare marbles—the remnants of the colonnades that once decked this magnificent palace of the most intellectual and civilised dynasty that Morocco ever boasted.

Reaching the Koutoubia Mosque, 1898
Robert Cunninghame Graham

It took us almost three-quarters of an hour to ride from the outside walls to the centre of the town. We passed through narrow lanes where camels jammed us almost to the walls; along the foot-paths beggars sat and showed their sores; dogs, yellow, ulcerous and wild as jackals, skulked between out horses' legs. At last we came out on an open space under the tower of the Kutubieh, in which square a sort of market was in progress, and a ring of interested spectators sat, crouched and stood, intent upon a story-teller's tale. I sat a moment listening on my horse, and heard enough to learn the story was after the style of the Arabian Nights, but quite unbowdlerized and suitable for Oriental taste.

Architecture of the Koutoubia, 1889
Walter Harris

The Koutoubia is the greatest of Marrakech's mosques, and universally commented upon. Those comments, always breathless, invariably include the news that the tower is sibling to those in Seville and Rabat, a wonderful illustration of the continuity of Moorish civilization across the Straits of Gibraltar.

The finest [minaret] by far is that of the Koutubia, or mosque of the booksellers, a minaret 250 feet in height and 50 feet square from base to summit. It is the sister tower to the Giralda at Seville, and the unfinished tower at Beni Hasan, at Rabat, but is finer than either, as the Giralda has undergone restoration and change at the hands of the Spaniards, whereas the Koutubia remains in its pristine glory. . . . To ascend the tower there are no stairs, but a sloping way, up which one could ride—so it is said—on horseback. No doubt the origin of this was to take the beasts of burden as near the working level as possible. This minaret, as it raises its head far above the low-lying town and the forests of palms, forms the landmark of Morocco. It was the first we saw of the city on our approach; it was the last we saw on our departure.

An African City, 1898
Robert Cunninghame Graham

The people are all African, men from the Draa, the Sus, the Sahara, Wad Nun and the mysterious sandy steps below Cape Bojador. . . . Tom-tom and gimbry are their chief instruments, together with the Moorish flute, ear-piercing and encouraging to horses, who when they hear its shriek step proudly, arching their necks and moving sideways down the streets as if they liked the sound. Their songs are African, the interval so strange and the rhythm so unlike that of all European music as at first hearing to be almost unintelligible; but at last grow on one until one likes them and endeavours to repeat their tunes.

Sand in the Diplomatic Uniform, 1889
Walter Harris

Harris was in the party of Sir William Kirby-Green, present-
ing his credentials to Sultan Hasan I.

Sand, sand and more sand in almost every street, in the
vast open spaces, in the long winding narrow lanes, outside the walls up to the city gates; sand in your hair, your
clothes, the coats of animals. Streets, streets, and still more
streets of houses in decay. Yellow adobe walls, dazzling
white roofs and dense metallic semi-tropical vegetation
shrouding the heaps of yellowish decaying masonry. No
noise, the footfalls of the mules and camels falling into the
sand as rain falls into the sea, with a soft swishing sound.

Questionable Personal Hygiene, 1860
James Richardson

The air of the country, at the foot of the Atlas, is pure and
salubrious. The city is well supplied from an aquaduct,
connecting it with the river Tensift, which flows from the

gorges of the Atlas. But the inhabitants, although they enjoy this inestimable blessing in an African climate, are not famous for their cleanliness.

Slavery through Rose-tinted Spectacles, 1889
Walter Harris

Like most Europeans, Harris was interested in the slave market. Predictably prurient, he is curiously unprepared to face the realities of enslavement.

We often visited the slave market, which is I think quite

the most interesting sight in Morocco. We had all read the fearful accounts which the press in Tangier is so fond of repeating . . . and I must confess, were most pleasantly surprised. We went often to the market but never saw such sights as children separated from their parents. . . . The slaves wore a wonderfully contented, even cheerful, expression while the sale was proceeding. We were much amused at watching one young lady—who, by the way, was rather handsome—alter her expression from sullenness when an old Moor was looking at her, to cheerfulness when a handsome young man began his inspection. . . . This I will say, that I would far rather be a slave in Morocco than a peasant. . . . It is not the slavery that is so bad, it is the kidnapping that slavery necessitates, and the terrible long journey over the scorching desert.

The Dark Comedy of a Reception by the Sultan, 1889
H.M.P. de la Martinière

But of course the epicenter of Marrakech (as at Fes), when he was in residence, was the sultan, and most accounts include

an audience with him. It was an affair of great if occasion-
ally ragged protocol, and diplomats in particular suffered the
agonies of thick serge uniforms under a blazing African sun.

The same ceremony, I was nearly saying the same comedy, is re-enacted with each important Embassy, and from the enthusiastic correspondence published, and the stereotyped despatches spread abroad, it would appear that, in every case, never in the memory of man was such a reception given, or could such a sympathetic concourse be remembered. The old Moghrebians who, in the course of their life, have been able to take part in a number of these wearisome ceremonies, would laugh uproariously if they read the comments which we in Europe make on such occasions.

Impertinent Treatment of British Diplomats, 1894
Stephen Bonsal

After keeping the Mission in quarantine for four days, as is prescribed by the etiquette of the Shereefian Court, the Sultan condescended to receive the British Envoy in the Meshwa. It must have been a repugnant sight—the British ambassador, an envoy plenipotentiary of her gracious Majesty, surrounded by his suite, standing bare-headed in the midday sun, awaiting the coming of the Black-a-Moor Sultan in the cool shade of an umbrella upon a prancing steed! Punctuality is not the practice of Mauretanian princes, at least, and in this humiliating situation, with the eyes of all Fez upon them, the Bashador and his suite were kept waiting . . . for fully half an hour.

An Imperial Reception for a New Ambassador, 1889
Walter Harris

So when Walter Harris describes the grand ambassadorial reception in which he took part, it is worth silently recalling both de la Martinière and Bonsal.

First, after a few kaids and the standard-bearer, rode Sir William and Lady Kirby-Green, followed by the ladies and official members of the expedition, and finally the "unofficialities". After having been on the road about ten minutes, our way led us between lines of mounted soldiers, who fell in as we passed along, increasing the dust, which was already terrible, for in spite of the early hour, the heat was intense. The scene was a very grand one and thoroughly Oriental, the procession headed by the vanguard, with the standard bearer in their midst carrying the Moorish red flag, once the terror of European trading-ships. A little further on the road was lined with infantry in scarlet and blue, and here we were met by Kaid Maclean, his brother, and the Basha of Morocco. As we passed the band of the regiment they struck up. What they played, no one could say; in fact, I think they did not stick to one tune, but each composed a little "morceau" of his own for the occasion. As we emerged from the palms into the open ground, the sight increased in gorgeousness, as the foot as well as the horsemen had fallen-in in our rear. The hot, dusty road with its soldiers in scarlet and blue, armed by the way with Winchester repeaters, the sun shining on the barrels and bayonets of the rifles, our own party half hidden in the clouds of yellow dust, the grey-walled town, with its minarets and palms, all formed a picture never to be forgotten. . . .

The Moors who were there to escort us to the presence of the Emperor were arrayed in soft haiks of snowy whiteness, from the graceful folds of which peeped the brilliant scarlets, greens and yellows of their kuftans, while the prancing, neighing horses added to the effect, each led by a soldier in scarlet and blue. . . .

At the gate of the Maimounieh we found a large escort waiting for us, as we passed through which trumpeters sounded a fanfare. After a minute's halt we were once more en route, our new escort having fallen-in in the rear. . . . Passing through two rather fine archways at each of which our approach was heralded by a blast of trumpets, we entered the great square of the Kasbah, into which the palace looks. The square we found full of troops; on our right and in front of us the infantry, on our left the cavalry, of which each man was dismounted, standing at his horse's head. It seemed almost incredible to us that Morocco could turn out so many soldiers, for we learned afterwards . . . that there were no less than twenty-two thousand men present. . . .

A blast of trumpets announced the Emperor and, the great gates being thrown open, the procession began to appear. First, led by black slaves, came four magnificent horses—a black, a grey, a bay and a white—following which marched the Court-Marshall with a white wand, various officials, spear-bearers and others; and finally the Sultan himself, mounted on a splendid horse, whose trappings of green and gold formed a strange contrast to the Emperor's plain white costume, which consisted of a jelab and haik, both of which were drawn over his turbaned head, no doubt as a protection from the sun, though this was scarcely needed, as high above him waved the Imperial umbrella, a marvellous structure of crimson and gold. On either side of His Majesty walked men whose duty it was to keep the flies off his sacred person by continually flapping the air with long white silk scarves.

The Bicycling Sultan, 1905
Gabriel Veyre

Of the court officials and hangers-on there are also fascinating accounts. Gabriel Veyre, the photographer, saw Moulay Abdel Aziz in conditions of great informality.

He was quite tall, and very fat, having all the makings of a giant but without the muscles. . . . Wanting to give him a bit of physical energy, [Kaid Maclean] advised the Sultan to take exercise. This was a novel distraction, which quite seduced Abdel Aziz. He ordered installed in a court of the palace a gymnastics beam with a trapeze; he learned leapfrog; practised with all the energy of which he was capable the gymnastics in use in the British army as well as tennis and football. . . . And one fine day he sat, for the first time, astride a bicycle. He took to it enthusiastically.

When I arrived in Marrakech, he used to pass his days on a bicycle. The Court of Amusements was transformed into a quite extraordinary race-course, furnished with obstacles, where we would hurl ourselves at the maddest fences, the Sultan, Maclean, el-Mehneby [the Minister of War], the English doctor Verdon and his brother, and one or two others.

On the course we normally followed, flattened, not very thick, boxes were arranged, and on them leaned narrow strips of plank, forming ramps for going up and down at each end. Next to these, boxes were piled one on another up to three or four feet from the ground; and then they were arranged in zig-zags, and steps were brought into the game, as were folding dinghies which Maclean had had brought from London and which became excellent piers for our vaulting bridges. Up there we had a large board where we made complicated figures, crossing, passing each other, doubling back. Alongside this we invented bicycle polo and at this we played on specially adapted machines with their wheels protected by sheets of celluloid to avoid the mallets getting into the spokes and risking an accident. At all these acrobatics the Sultan was extraordinarily good, without flattery the best of us all. To begin with his long clothes, his djellaba, got in the way a little so we proposed to him, for his convenience, that he ride a lady's bicycle. But when he discovered that it was a machine constructed specially for the weaker sex he rebelled proudly.

A Golden Camera for the Sultan, 1905
Gabriel Veyre

Of all the pastimes to which, one after another, he devoted himself, it was [photography] which amused

Abdel Aziz for longest, and gave him the most satisfaction. He acquired an uncommon skill at it. . . . He was not satisfied, like so many amateurs, even imperial or royal amateurs, simply to press the button, to release the shutter. He wanted to be initiated into all the delicate procedures of the laboratory.

. . . He dreamed of an extraordinary camera, one beyond equal. The little vérascope, so easy to handle, so practical, had won his favour above all. He wanted me to make him one entirely out of gold, and he wanted it so imperiously that, despite my explaining the difficulties of such a work, I went to work to give him his satisfaction, and in due course he had his vérascope, specially made for him in Paris by skilled artisans, all in gold and stamped with the official French hall-mark; the only parts not pure gold were made of steel, gilt steel: a fantasy which must have cost him twenty-five thousand francs.

Ordinary photography, already quite complicated and rich in possibilities, wasn't good enough for him, and when he heard tell of color photography, he wanted to have a go at that. I taught him the technique with three colors, and when he had mastered that, he spent long days, shut in his harem, photographing his wives. Because it was ultimately his ambition to capture once and for all, their forms and characters.

He had them wear their most spectacular costumes, jewels, collars, bracelets, brooches; he put them in front of a background of the most luminous carpets and arranged around them, on a table draped with the busiest of cloths, artificial flowers of the most extravagant and garish sort and tried then to take the most highly-colored pictures that he could arrange.

A Visit to the Harem, 1793
William Lemprière

William Lemprière attended an earlier sultan in order to treat his wives for a variety of ailments. Here he visits the senior lady of the harem.

I found Lalla Batoom to be a perfect Moorish beauty; she was most immoderately fat, about forty years of age, with round and prominent cheeks, which were painted a deep red, small black eyes, and a visage completely guiltless of expression. She was sitting upon a mattress on the floor which, as usual, was covered with fine white linen, and she was surrounded by a large party of concubines, whom I was informed she had invited to be her visitors on the occasion.

As soon as I entered her apartment, Lalla Batoom requested me to be seated close by her side, and to feel her pulse. Her complaint was a slight cold, of which an unconquerable desire of seeing me had most probably been the occasion. As soon as I had felt her pulse, and pronounced my opinion, I was employed in going through the same ceremony with all the other ladies in the room, who desired I would acquaint them with all their complaints, without any further enquiries. From . . . the knowledge which I had attained of their complaints, which in general proceeded from too violent an attack upon the Coscosoo [couscous], I was enabled to make no despicable figure in this mysterious art, and was very successful in my opinions.

Female Delicacy and Indelicacy, 1793
William Lemprière

As the female sex in this country are not entrusted with the guardianship of their own honour, there is no virtue in reserve. A depraved education even serves to corrupt instead of to restrain them. They are not regarded as rational or moral agents; they are only considered as beings created entirely to be subservient to the pleasures of man. To excite the passions, and to do and say every thing which may inflame a licentious imagination, become therefore necessary accomplishments of the female sex, and their manners and conduct naturally assume a cast totally different from those of women in a more refined and more liberal state of society. In those instances to which I refer, they were not conscious of trespassing the limits of decency; and in others they manifested a singular attention to what they conceived as decorum. When I requested to see the tongues of some patients who complained of feverish symptoms, they refused to comply, considering it as inconsistent with their modesty and virtue.

Essaouira

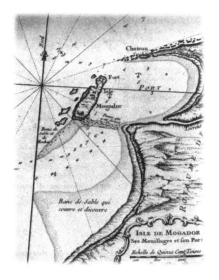

Known for centuries by its Portuguese name, Mogador, Essaouira is the port of Marrakech, though today it is probably at least as famous in its reincarnation as Astapor, the city on Slaver's Bay in Game of Thrones. *It was founded*

by Sultan Sidi Muhammad ben Abdallah in 1764, a move
designed to concentrate the trade of the kingdom in one port,
under his fiscal eye. It has an astonishing climate, much cooler
than Marrakech, often windblown, generally delightful. This
is a huge relief as one approaches the coast in summer from
the blazing heat of Marrakech.

Its Name Is Perfection, 1879
Charles Payton

The British Consul in the 1880s, Charles Payton, who was
stout and disliked intense heat, flourished here.

We have a climate here—its name is perfection. *Weather*
we have none; it is, except during the short season of
winter, always bright and sunshiny, always warm, never
hot—"a land where it is always afternoon."

One of the most delightful of all essays on Morocco is Nicholas
Shakespeare's Journey to the End of the World, *published*
in the Telegraph Magazine *in October 1993. The author*

sets out in search of Mogador's past, traces of Payton, and above all memories of this once intensely Jewish city. Many of Mogador's Jews were British subjects, naturalized in Gibraltar and so the charge of the British consul. Shakespeare's quest was for the Jewish antecedents of Leslie Hore-Belisha, British Secretary of State for War, whose Belisha family were said to have been natives of the city. The Jews of old Mogador imported from Manchester cornflower blue cotton cloth, dyed to the taste of the Tuareg who came trading from Timbuktu and the Niger bend. To exchange for the usual trans-Saharan exotics, of gum, ivory, and feathers, the ships from Manchester brought not just cotton, but tea, silver plate, and other 'Manishista' wares, including, as Shakespeare reports, "thousands of bowler hats. 'All the Jews wore bowlers.' Corcos reckons there were 9,000 of them. The bowlers made up half the population and the cafes lilted with English accents." It was said that Mogador was closer to Manchester than to Fes, and Payton's Vice-Consul, R.N.L. Johnson, wrote that "A certain foreign gentle man wanted, ironically, to know if Mogador belonged to the Sultan or to Queen Victoria. The response, with hand on heart, was 'Bijujhum ya senor'—to both, sir."

The Founding of Mogador, 1793
William Lemprière

Mogadore, so named by the Europeans, and Suera by the Moors, is a large, uniform and well-built town. . . . It was raised under the auspices of the late emperor, who upon his accession to the throne, ordered all the European merchants who were settled in his dominions to reside at Mogadore, where, by lowering the duties, he promised to afford every encouragement to commerce. The Europeans, thus obliged to desert their former establishments, considering this first step of the emperor to be a mark of his attachment to trade and commerce, and having resided long in the country without any better views at home, universally settled at Mogadore, where they erected houses, and other conveniences for the purpose of trade. The hopes, however, with which they had changed their situation, were considerably frustrated by the perfidy of the emperor, who indeed fulfilled his promise, till he observed the merchants so fixed as not to be likely to remove; but he then began to increase the duties, and by that means to damp the spirit of commerce which he had promised to promote.

The Beauties of Mogador, 1793
William Lemprière

Essaouira was, and remains, a pretty place, a walled town by the sea with breakers crashing on the sea-walls. It is more peaceful today than in Lemprière's time, when it was new and strange to its neighbours.

Mogadore is regularly fortified on the sea side; and on the land side batteries are so placed as to prevent any incursion from the southern Arabs, who are of a turbulent disposition, and who, from the great wealth that is known always to be in Mogadore, would gladly avail themselves of any opportunity that offered to pillage the town. The entrance, both by sea and land, consists of elegant stone archways with double gates. The market-place is handsomely built, with piazzas of the same materials, and at the water-port there is a custom house and powder magazine, both of which are neat stone buildings. Beside these public edifices, the emperor has a small but handsome palace for his occasional residence. The streets of the town, though very narrow, are all in strait lines, and the houses, contrary to what we meet with in the other towns of the empire, are lofty and regular. The bay, which is little better than a road, and is very much exposed when the wind is at North-West, is formed by a curve in the land, and a small island about a quarter of a mile from the shore.

The Patagonian Consul, 1898
Robert Cunninghame Graham

As Nicholas Shakespeare's title implies, Mogador did seem rather like the end of the world. Cunninghame Graham describes the beginning of a diplomatic entanglement that illustrates its remoteness and ignorance nicely.

It seemed that about eighteen months ago, one Abdel Kerim Bey, an Austrian subject, had arrived and hoisted his flag as Patagonian consul. Brazil and Portugal, Andorra, San Marino, Guatemala, Haiti and San Domingo, Siam, the Sandwich Islands, Kotei, Acheen, the Transvaal, Orange Free State, and almost any place where there was revenue sufficient to buy a flag and issue postage stamps for philatelists, had long ago sent consuls to Mogador. Their flag-staffs reared aloft like a mighty canebrake, from the sea; their banners shaded the streets after the fashion of the coverings which the Romans drew over their amphitheatres, and half the population were consuls of some semi-bankrupt state. Yet Patagonia, even in Mogador, excited some surprise. Jews who had been in Buenos Ayres (and a considerable quantity emigrate there from Mogador) argued that Patagonia was under the authority of the Argentine Republic. . . . The Arabs, whose geography is fragmentary, thought "Batagonia" was situated somewhere in Franguestan, and that contented them. What struck their fancy most was certainly the colour and design of the new oriflamme. Barred white and blue, a rising sun grinning across three mountain tops, a cap of liberty and a huanaco ruminant; an Araucanian Indian in his war-paint in one corner, and here and there stars, daggers, scales and other democratic trade-marks, made up a banner the like of which had seldom been observed in all the much be-bannered town of Mogador. The owner of this standard and the defender in Morocco of the lives and liberties of Patagonian subjects, dressed like a Turk (long single-breasted black frock coat and fez), and spoke a little Turkish but no Arabic.

A Consular Fishing Trip, 1879
Charles Payton

Payton clearly loved Mogador, though he remained obstinately English. Here he describes departing from the harbour in a small boat, on a fishing trip.

Stately Moors of the better class, officers of the port and of the customs, in snowy turbans and *haiks*, and clean yellow slippers, looked gravely on, or exchanged greetings and courtesies of infinite dignity with their acquaintances among the European population.

Getting on board a roomy four-oared boat, in company with the Jewish ship's interpreter, a Moorish port officer, a couple of rams, sundry cackling chickens, some huge water melons and a basket of grapes as big as plums, I contemplated the bright scene with considerable pleasure, as the bronzed and sinewy boatmen bent to their oars, chanting the while strange melodies of barbaric rhythm.

Threading the intricate and dangerous maze of rocks which make the entrance to the little dock of Mogador impassable save to craft of light draught, we soon left the white, blue and brown *omnium gatherum* of humanity on shore far behind.; and I gazed on the beautiful town, with its brown battlements, white houses, many flagstaffs, lofty mosques with green-tiled minarets, and felt a certain pang of regret at leaving.

Meknes

Moulay Ismail, the ferocious, effective, and psychopathic sultan who effectively founded the Alaouite dynasty, demolished (as we have seen) the palace of his predecessors at Marrakech and, not content with a new palace, founded a new capital city. This is Meknes, not far from Fes, the place where the sultan had been born, now magnified out of all propor-

tion. Meknes—or Mequinez—is the child of one man, not an organic growth but the project of a single long reign. Contemporary with Versailles, as Ismail was with Louis XIV, it is a spectacular city, megalomaniac in its stagey grandeur, blood-soaked in its construction by Christian slaves. Though it outlived its founder, it remained and remains the most 'junior' of the Imperial Cities, huge, impressive, and yet somehow insubstantial. In Budgett Meakin's terse summary: "Least imposing of the three imperial cities, hardly metropolitan in character, Mequinez has nonetheless its special interests. . . . Here Ismail the bloodthirsty held his court, and here, in the days when Moorish pirates swept the seas, the European captives fared their worst."

An Ambassador Arrives, 1694
François Pidou de Saint Olon

Saint Olon, French ambassador to Moulay Ismail, certainly didn't think much of the town, though he was delighted by the enormous palace.

The sultan has his ordinary residence at Meknes, because it is his birthplace. It is a small town in the countryside forty leagues from Salé, sixty from Tetouan and twelve from Fes; it is well populated, with more than sixty thousand inhabitants, but is so badly built and so disagreeable that it would seem no more than a mean little town were it not for its large population, the presence of the Prince—and the ornamentation of its palace the extent of which is not much smaller than that of the city itself. The palace itself is far above what I could possibly have imagined in the light of all the other buildings I have seen in this country.

What one sees on arriving at Meknes is the palace set above the city, encircled by many walls, all very tall, very thick and very white, made up of many pavilions and above them the tall minarets of its two mosques. These give a fine impression, but it is not substantiated on coming closer: everything is built with so little art and so little regularity that it would be difficult for the most experienced architects to disentangle its function and design. I even believe, to judge by what I have seen from outside (because I wasn't permitted to enter), that the king himself, its author and builder, would not be able to explain it. In fact I suspect that he has no other plan in what he continually demolishes and rebuilds than to oppress with the yoke of servitude and work the huge number of his subjects he employs.

This work is the occupation, and the normal torment, of Christian slaves who the king makes work at all times and without respite. They are forced to work as laborers and stone-masons by beatings and misery, to which they give way all the more easily because their daily diet consists of no more than a tiny quantity of black barley bread, with water; and because they only lay their heads in the *matamorres* or underground caverns, in which they have no bed but the hard earth, and breathe only foul air well mixed with evil smells.

Audience with Moulay Ismail, 1694
François Pidou de Saint Olon

We all went on foot to the audience, though it was a long road we had to walk. The heat was great, but I was furnished with a parasol which was some help against the sun's rays, very strong in this country. A dozen French slaves walked behind my party, carrying the presents that I had to give to the king of Morocco in my own name—fine weapons, expensive watches, many bolts of red and blue cloth, rich brocades of silver and gold, and two carpets from the Savonnerie of unique size and beauty.

So we entered the Alcazar, the king's palace, by a large and beautiful gateway called, for the two marble columns in front of it, the Marble Gate. Having followed a long avenue, lined on left and right by negroes of the Royal Guard and shut off on both sides by high, white walls made only (like all those of the palace) of lime, plaster, and cement that, beaten together by men's hands, made a material as hard as marble, and very white. We arrived at a half-built and unroofed pavilion made of four large porticos, each facing a similar avenue, serving as roads to the different lodgings of this Alcazar.

I was made to stop at the entrance, to wait there, I was told, while someone warned the king of my arrival. It was a full quarter of an hour before he appeared, coming down one of the avenues, which was bordered by a hedge of two hundred or so little negroes with huge muskets, which they lowered almost to the ground as he passed.

He had a small retinue and rode a white horse, very different in beauty and richness of harness from the one on which I had seen him on the day of the review. In his hand he held a lance, or long pike, and beyond the fact that he was dressed as simply as the least of his subjects, his face was covered as far as his eyes by a coffee-colored handkerchief, which looked fairly dirty and made a rather poor effect.

He set foot on the ground at the entry to this portico, and having given his lance to one of his negroes he came and sat, without mat or rug, on the edge of a great wooden post, which served as a buttress. His arms and his legs were naked, and a negro carried a fan behind him to give him some fresh air, and to drive away the flies, which are many and tiresome in that country.

Calling on Moulay Ismail, 1721
John Windus

Windus accompanied the British ambassador Commodore Stewart.

Ben Hattar (by the emperor's order) conducting us to see the palace, we were led into a large oblong-square building, with piazzas all round, being the Queen of the Xeriph's apartment. The arches were wrought with plaster fret-work, in flowers after the Arabian manner, and supported by neat stone pillars; the square exceeding large and spacious; the bottom and sides (for about five feet high) chequered with small tiles of divers colours, about two inches square; of which small chequer-work there is a prodigious quantity in the palace.

All the apartments, walks, magazines, passages, and underneath the arches being chequered, making the prospect of the buildings, which are all of a great length, extremely magnificent, beautiful and neat. From thence we were led into a magazine near a quarter of a mile long, and not above thirty feet broad; in it there hung up great quantities of arms in cases, and three rows of rails, which were covered with saddles, almost from one end to the other: and in such another magazine they shewed us the gates of Larach, which this Emperor took from the Spaniards, a great deal of iron-work, some espadas, and other Christian swords, brought from thence. Then we were carried into another large and spacious building, with piazzas all round like the former. In this live two of the Emperor's wives, who are distinguished by being called the Queens of the Cobah 'lhodrah, (which is the name of that part of the palace they live in) and are in great esteem with him.

From thence passing through some neat long walks and passages of chequer-work, we came to another building, with a large garden in the middle, planted round with tall cypress trees: the garden is sunk about sixty or seventy feet lower than the foundation of the building, over which, from one side to the other, goes a terrace-walk, called by the Moors the Strangee, which is about half a mile long, and fifteen or sixteen feet broad; the top of it all the way thick-shaded with vines, and other greens, supported with strong and well-made wooden work. In this walk there was a chariot that goes with springs, and a small calash, in which they told us the Emperor is sometimes drawn by women and eunuchs.

Several other squares and long buildings we passed through, now and then seeing the Christians upon the top of high walls, working and beating down the mortar with heavy pieces of wood, (something like what our paviers used to beat down the stones) which they raise all together, and keep time in their stroke; and after we had been about three hours seeing the palace, we were led again to the Emperor, who was on horseback, at the entrance of a cobah, in which were stores of arms, lances, and other things, kept in order by twenty-eight English boys.

A Great Ghost Town, 1890
Pierre Loti

A later French traveler, Pierre Loti, was struck, like Saint Olon, by the dramatic flimsiness of Meknes and its carefully designed beauty.

Emerging from these walls and olive trees, suddenly Mékinez appeared, very close to us and appearing enormous, crowning with its dark shape a line of hills behind which the sun was setting. We were separated from the town only by a green ravine filled with poplars, blackberries, orange trees, odd shrubs run wild, all with their lush April colors. Very high up, against the yellowing heavens, were the outlines of one rampart above another, countless terraces, minarets, mosque towers, strong crenelated casbahs, and then above the many fortress walls, the roof of green-glazed tiles on the sultan's palace. It is even more imposing than Fez, and more solemn. But it is just a great ghost town, a cluster of ruins and decay where hardly five thousand people live—Arabs, Berbers, and Jews.

During the long midday halt, our people told us that we would arrive in time for the sunset prayer. And indeed, just as we appeared, the white flag of prayer was raised on every minaret—the Allahu Akbar rang out in a terrifying clamor right across the holy city as far as the dead lands around it . . . and in these long, lugubrious cries this Allah, to whom these men were appealing, seemed to us at that moment, so great and so terrible that we too would have liked to prostrate ourselves on the earth, answering the call of the mouedzins, in the face of his sombre eternity.

The Slave Bagnios, 1889
Walter Harris

Under the pavements of Meknes are vast vaulted cellars, reputedly the bagnios in which the slaves were kept. Harris describes them with his usual panache.

Close to the tomb of Moulai Ismail, under the open square, are a great series of subterranean vaults, as inexplicable as most of the ruins of Mequinez. We descended, as I had done once before. One "glissades" down; the first time I glissaded down I alighted on the skeleton of a camel and bruised my knee, this time on the decomposing carcase of a cow. It was softer, but I preferred the camel. These dungeons extend to a great distance, the roof being supported by massive columns; the long black arcades in which flit the squeaking bats, and the refreshing odour of carcases in every stage of decay have inspired the Moors with awe, and the popular belief is that these vaults are the residence of many a "djin" and devil.

"The Two Most Fanatical Sects," 1889
Walter Harris

With an eye for drama and religious excess, Harris describes the two religious zaouias with their centres at Meknes.

As Mequinez is the seat of the two most fanatical sects of the Mohammedan religion in Morocco, I will here describe, as far as I can, their religious rites.

These two sects are respectively the Aissoui and the Hamdouchi. The former are the followers of Sidi Ben Aissa, whose remains rest at Mequinez, as do those of Sidi Ali Ben Hamdouch, the patron saint of the other order. . . .

Whoever Sidi Ben Aissa may have been, we know what power he is said to have possessed, viz. that of rendering harmless the bite of snakes and reptiles to those who are his followers. Any one, any Mohammedan, can become an Aissoui. The inauguration is simple. He journeys to Mequinez, calls upon the present representative of Sidi Ben Aissa's family, to whom he offers prayers and money—especially money. This over, the priest blows on him, and the devotee arises and sets out in the firmest belief that however many venomous snakes may bite him, however many scorpions sting him, no harm will befall. How discomforting the illusion must be at times! The believer who sits down upon a scorpion soon discovers that he has given the priest of the Aissouis more power than he is justified in receiving—and more money. . . .

The rites of the Hamdouchis much resemble those of their fellow sect, though instead of preserving them from snake-bites, they are enabled to wound themselves without suffering any after result.

I will not enter fully into the details of a Hamdouchi festival, as the sight is too loathsome even to describe, and it will be sufficient, I think, to say, that when in a state of frenzy they cut their heads open with fast-falling self-inflicted blows of battle-axes, and gash their bodies with knives. I have seen Hamdouchis, stark naked, covered with blood, blue in the face and foaming at the mouth, their head a network of long cuts, and daggers passing through their cheeks, rolling in the sand and biting stones. . . .

Another favourite pastime of the Hamdouchis is to throw cannonballs and heavy stones into the air and to allow them to fall upon their clean-shaven heads with a thud that would knock the brains out of most men.

Ease of Travel and Safety at Meknes, 1889
H.M.P. de la Martinière

By the late nineteenth century, though, it was an easy enough destination, and de la Martinière comments that . . .

I spent two months there in absolute quietude, and except for the confounded trumpets of the Muezzins nightly reminding the faithful of the dinner hour, during this season of gladness, and the nocturnal feasts of the

Ramadan, I could have lived there perfectly happy. . . . not a shadow of anything disagreeable ever came near us, whether we were attired in an English travelling suit or in a comfortable "djellaba." . . . I have been able, alone, and without any escort, to photograph all the most interesting nooks and corners.

And no falling cannon balls.

Rabat

The modern capital of Morocco, Rabat is a city of great charm and beauty, though being heavily developed. A French resident in the 1920s wrote that "for the moment, Rabat still guards its special character . . . that of a small, elegant provincial town where one is always happy to recover in the calm of privileged nature, green, and still full of the poetic memories of past ages." Amazingly, it remains so. Its history

is strange—a vast, empty circuit of walls built, but never turned into the city he imagined, by Sultan Yaqub al-Mansour in the twelfth century, filled only by the French in the twentieth. It spent the intervening years confined to the small medina on the point, alternately pirate republic and backwater. Rabat acquired its special character with the influx of Moriscos from Spain after their final expulsion in 1614; and this cultural transfusion gave rise to more than a century of 'revenge-piracy' as well as to the very particular Andalusian culture of Rabat, which did much to shape the high culture of Morocco as a whole. Lying across the mouth of the Bouregreg river from Salé, it is often paired with its older neighbour, and development has today turned them effectively into one great city.

Arriving from Fes by Motor-car, 1920
Edith Wharton

Speeding along through the stunted cork-trees of the forest of Mamora brought us to a last rise from which we beheld in the dusk a line of yellow walls backed by the misty blue of the Atlantic. Salé, the fierce old pirate town, where Robinson Crusoe was so long a slave, lay before us, snow-white in its cheese-coloured ramparts skirted by fig and olive gardens. Below its gates a stretch of waste land, endlessly trailed over by mules and camels, sloped down to the mouth of the Bou-Regreg, the blue-brown river dividing it from Rabat. The motor stopped at the landing-stage of the steam-ferry; crowding about it were droves of donkeys, knots of camels, plump-faced merchants on crimson-saddled mules, with negro servants at their bridles, bare-legged water-carriers with hairy goat-skins slung over their shoulders, and Arab women in a heap of veils, cloaks, mufflings, all of the same ashy white, the caftans of clutched children peeping through in patches of old rose and lilac and pale green.

Across the river the native town of Rabat lay piled up on an orange-red cliff beaten by the Atlantic. Its walls, red too, plunged into the darkening breakers at the mouth of the river; and behind it, stretching up to the mighty tower of Hassan, and the ruins of the Great Mosque, the scattered houses of the European city showed their many lights across the plain.

The Merchants of Rabat, 1920
Edith Wharton

Everything that the reader of the Arabian Nights expects to find is here: the whitewashed niches wherein pale youths sit weaving the fine mattings for which the town is still famous; the tunnelled passages where indolent merchants with bare feet crouch in their little kennels hung with richly ornamented saddlery and arms, or with slippers of pale citron leather and bright embroidered babouches; the stalls with fruit, olives, tunny-fish, vague syrupy sweets, candles for saints' tombs, Mantegnesque garlands of red and green peppers, griddle-cakes sizzling on red-hot pans, and all the varied cakes and condiments that the lady in the tale of 'The Three Calendars' went out to buy, that memorable morning, in the market of Bagdad.

A French Warship Arrives at Rabat, 1910
Ellis Ashmead-Bartlett

The roar of the guns brought the people from their homes and the warriors from their camp to foregather on the hills, which, rising straight up from the water, oppose a rocky rampart to the intruder, and from there to gaze in wonder and admiration on the warship. Her crew leaning over the rails in idle curiosity saw before them a scene of surprising barbaric splendour. They gazed on Sali, its thick walls dotted with cannon, which glowered from embrasures centuries old; on its white, flat-topped houses and tall minarets, the whole sullen and aloof, separated from more tolerant Rabat by the angry bar at the river's mouth. For centuries Sali has remained the same, an enemy of Christianity and civilisation, and still the most fanatical town in Morocco, just as Robinson Crusoe found it when held there a prisoner for two years by the Barbary pirates before setting out on his historic voyage. The Atlantic rollers breaking in cascades of spray at the mouth of the river mark the bar; then comes Rabat, standing as its sentinel, a jumble of rock forts and houses, nature and man's work difficult to distinguish. The hills which front the ocean are thickly dotted with the tombs of former generations of the faithful. Beneath the soil lie those who laughed at the infidel and bade him defiance from the walls of the sacred city,—men who were accustomed to charge their cannons with shot, not to salute strangers as welcome guests. The tombs remain, but the spirit of the heroic age has fled, the bow of Allah is unstrung and the faithful wander ashamed amidst the scenes of their former glory. The hills beyond are spread with white tents clustering round a great striped one, the home of the Sultan when on the march. Beyond, and towering over all, stands the Hassan tower, emblem of a great Sultan who did rule, crumbling with neglect, but still upright amidst the general decay of mind and matter. Among the tents, houses and tombs the Sultan's warriors wandered, and wondered what the presence of the great warship could mean.

The Bouregreg Estuary and Its Perils, 1906
Louis Mercier

Mercier, French vice-consul in Rabat, describes the estuary and the sandbar that created, in the right tidal conditions, the lethal turbulence that had protected the Bouregreg as a pirate refuge, and which still caused fatal disasters at the turn of the last century.

You notice all day right up until sunset, a lively coming and going between Rabat and Salé. Travelers include native merchants of Salé who have their warehouses in Rabat and are on their way there; many women who go to sell woollen thread or silk embroidery in one of the two markets; the peasants of one bank who have business on the other and bring their wares, by donkey, mule, or camel; and notables of the neighboring tribes who come on horseback to talk to the qaid, to buy cloth for their women or to furnish themselves with rifle cartridges or other small purchases.

To get to Salé from Rabat, you leave by Bab El-Behar in the eastern wall and you find yourself on a small beach strewn with large flat rocks, which the sea reveals as the tide goes out. Here there are many boats of all sizes, some only for carrying foot passengers, others able to carry loaded donkeys, sheep, goats, and cows; and yet others that can take mules, horses, and camels with their loads. It is a strange sight to be present at the embarkation of an obstinate mule or a frightened camel. The ferryman grabs one leg of the animal that is to embark and pulls it upward until it upsets the animal's balance. He is helped in this by the owner who shouts at his frightened beast until it jumps into the boat. You will also see horses and mules used to crossing regularly, which jump unprompted into the boat with great aplomb.

The ferryman rows standing in the bow of his boat, facing the direction of travel and using two big oars. There is no rudder. The current, of which the direction varies according to the tide, is often very strong and pushes many boats off their course. It even happens, if the boatman doesn't know his trade, that a boat is driven onto the bar and capsized by large waves. In this sort of case, many passengers don't make it back to shore.

The further you get from the river bank, the better and more picturesque is the view, the houses seeming to be piled up on the lip of the steep rocky cliff, except around the Customs House which is almost level with the water. The Qaçba, with its imposing fortifications and its crumbling walls crowned with greenery, makes a marvelous sight.

Arriving on the right bank, the boats beach on a sandy bottom, and you must walk another five or six hundred meters across golden sand, depending on the tide, to reach the walls of Salé. On this side, they are partly hidden by greenery and gardens.

The Mellah, 1906
Louis Mercier

Like every Moroccan city, Rabat had its mellah, the gated Jewish ghetto, perhaps named for the salt—malh—with which the Jews had once been required to pickle the detached heads of the sultan's enemies.

The Jewish quarter . . . is formed by a large central street off which lead many cul-de-sacs. At the end of this main street, on the west side, there is a large open space, up against the southern and eastern faces of the inner walls. This is where the great rubbish heaps of the quarter, which is remarkable for its cleanliness, are located. Here too blow the foul stenches of various local industries, the drying of bones after butchering, of animal waste, and of skins. A large breach opened in the walls on the eastern side very close to the southeast angle gives onto the river and Salé, offering a magnificent view. This breach has never been sealed up again, undoubtedly through the negligence of the Makhzen, and perhaps also because the cliff here constitutes an adequate natural defence, overlooking the waters of the river with an almost vertical drop of about fifteen meters. At the entrance to the Mellah are to be found the butcheries for kosher meat and the spice and vegetable merchants. All along the main street there are the shops of tailors, shoe-makers, silk-workers, embroiderers on leather, tinsmiths, and so on.

Gunfire and Tennis at the Hasan Tower, 1906
Louis Mercier

Beyond the Andalusian Wall—the inland wall of the Rabat medina—lay wasteland stretching up the hill to the two great extra-mural monuments, the Hasan Tower and the Chellah, or Shella. These were the destinations of regular excursions, though in Mercier's day not entirely safe, suffering regular raids by tribesmen.

Very few citizens dare to venture as far as the Hasan Tower, because its position close to the Oued, on the edge of which there is no rampart at all, means that one can all too easily meet there Za'er or Zemmour tribesmen with hostile intentions. On the other hand the tower is the destination of a walk much used by Europeans, though it is true that they usually go there in a group, accompanied by guards and themselves well armed. . . .

The remains of enormous walls, ten meters high, enclose a large square space. In this space still stand a good many marble columns, made up of superimposed marble cylinders some sixty centimeters long. Other columns lie on the ground, but most have been removed to serve in the construction of other, more recent buildings. All this must have been the mosque of which the Hasan Tower was the minaret. It stands on the north edge of the ruins, sixty-five meters high. From an architectural point of view it is very interesting, and seems to have been built to the same plans as the Giralda at Seville and the Koutoubya of Marrakech. Hunters appreciate it for other reasons: they come to shoot the innumerable pigeons which are, these days, the only inhabitants of this grand monument. It is in this setting, between the columns that still stand and what remains of the western wall, that the European colonies have chosen to install a tennis court. Once used every day, this tennis court is now deserted, security these days being inadequate.

The Waters and Sanctuaries of Chellah, 1906
Louis Mercier

Chellah is one of Rabat's great glories, a necropolis built by Sultan Abul Hassan Ali on the site of a Roman port whose forum and baths still stand there, and beneath which perhaps lies the first, Carthaginian, settlement. Surrounded by spectacular walls, it is a shrine, a paradise of storks, and a garden for Rbatis from the city, teeming with families on a Friday. It has a pool of sacred eels, from which the barren ladies of Rabat seek fertility, and of which Nina Epton records that "a queenly eel is said to rule over all the creatures of Chella that share her small watery domain . . . a queenly eel with long hair and ear-rings." Mercier is more prosaic.

The monumental gate of Chella is no more than five hundred meters in a straight line from Bab El-Hadid. Flanked by two bastions it is, like Chella as a whole, one of the most interesting features of the whole area from an architectural and archaeological point of view. The northwest angle of the enclosure is the one that has suffered most damage.

Over and above the numerous mausoleums and sanctuaries inside it, Chella offers to researchers the remarkable remains of a lovely mosque. Very close to it you can see the works that collect and store the waters of the spring that supplies water to rich citizens. Unfortunately, the complete absence of security as soon as you leave the first circuit of Rabat's walls means that it is rarely possible to go to Chella and devote the time which it deserves, to studying it.

The Gardens of Chellah, 1816
Ali Bey al-Abbassi

Ali Bey perhaps visited on a Friday, when still today on a fine afternoon the Roman forum is crowded with families.

As well as the tombs and picnickers he was struck by the gardens, which though much changed are still lovely.

At the eastern part of the town the remains of the ancient town of Shella are to be seen: Mr Chenier supposes it to have been the metropolis of the Carthaginian colonies. Leon calls this town Sallæ. . . . Shella is surrounded by very high walls, and no Christian is admitted into the town; which contains the sepulchres of several saints; that of El-Mansur is placed in a handsome and much frequented mosque. The day when I went there, it was so much crowded with women, that I found much difficulty in getting in. The descent of the hill, at the foot of which this mosque is situated, is really romantic, from numerous cascades of bright water precipitating itself between rocks, amid rose-bushes, orange and lemon trees, and numberless aromatic flowers. After I left the mosque, I took a walk in the orange gardens which border the river; they may with truth be called an earthly paradise. The trees, always covered with blossom and fruit, afford a delightful fragrance, and the most delicate refreshment, which, being within reach, may be enjoyed on the spot. The orange trees are so thick, so large, and so tufted, that walking under them even in the middle of the day, they afford shelter against the effects of the sun, and I have found no where in Europe any gardens which have afforded me so much delight as those of Rabat.

Fortifications and Female Beauties, 1793
William Lemprière

The town of Rabat, whose walls enclose a large space of ground, is defended on the sea side by three forts tolerably well finished, which were erected some time ago by an English renegade and furnished with guns from Gibraltar. The houses in general are good, and many of the inhabitants are wealthy. The Jews, who are very numerous in this place, are generally in better circumstances than those of Larache or Tangier, and their women are by far more beautiful than at any other town which I saw in this empire. I was introduced to one family in particular, where, out of eight sisters, Nature had been so lavish to them all, that I felt myself at a loss to determine which was the handsomest. A combination of regular features, clearness of complexion, and expressive black eyes, gave them a distinguished pre-eminence over their nation in general; and their persons, though not improved by the advantages which the European ladies derive from dress, were still replete with grace and elegance.

The Decline of Piracy, 1816
Ali Bey al-Abbassi

This place has nothing of its ancient maritime splendour, but three or four captains who are scarcely capable of governing a large ship; and if the Sultan were to arm ships of a large size, he would find it difficult to meet with proper men to command them. If, however, maritime skill were only to renew their former taste for pirating, it is happier for Europe that they never think of improving in this art.

Moriscos and the Survival of Learning, 1816
Ali Bey al-Abbassi

The inhabitants are lively, intelligent and with more imagination than those of the other towns. There are some families who boast of descending from Spanish refugees, who at several periods arrived in Africa, and have not changed their names. One of them, of the name of Sidi Matte Moreno, is the only learned man of the empire who has any knowledge of astronomy; it is of a very ancient sort, but it is, however, founded on good principles.

Lyautey Arrives at Rabat and Is Horrified, 1931
André Maurois

It was the French resident-general, Maréchal Lyautey, who set the standards for French urbanism in Morocco, and while there is much to regret, Lyautey's romantic attachment to traditional Moorish cityscapes and urban life did at least protect a great deal of what existed in 1912 and which we can still see today.

They set off on horseback for Rabat. The Kasbah of the Oudaias, a hill of white cubes, shone peacefully in the sunlight near the Arab cemetery. The engineers had already started building barracks of the conventional type. Lyautey burst into one of his fierce rages. Was this beautiful native town to be ruined by these hideous official constructions? In this fresh new country he was going to find the zinc washing-places, the black strip along the bottom of the flaking whitewashed walls, the smell of coal-tar. "Heavens above!" he cried. "Can't you pull that down and wait for my plans?" No, the engineers could not pull it down. They had already spent 150,000 francs. Lyautey gave orders for the work of construction to be held up . . . and proceeded on his way towards Fez.

Tangier

Before air travel, Tangier was the gateway of Morocco for Europeans. Fourteen miles from Spain, it was easily reached by ferry, but seemed the beginning of another world. It was the European focus of Morocco, the epicenter of penetration,

peaceful and otherwise, the exile of sultans, and the disreputable pleasure-ground of Europeans. Between the wars it had an international administration, outside the French and Spanish protectorate. It is a strange and perhaps unique place. But it had a previous life that gives it a special interest for the British: for twenty-three years in the late seventeenth century, it was a possession of the English crown, of which Samuel Pepys wrote with premature optimism that "Tangier is likely to be the most considerable place the King of England has in the world." Forming part of the dowry of Catherine of Braganza when she married Charles II in 1661, it saw a half-hearted and ultimately unsuccessful attempt to build a great British trading-port at the mouth of the Mediterranean. After two decades, the British garrison withdrew in the face of Moorish attack, blew up the enormous and hugely expensive harbor mole, and sailed away.

Arriving at Tangier by Sea, 1675
George Philips

On *Saturday* the 12 of *June* [1675], early in the morning, we entred the Passage into the *Streights*, between

Cape Spartel and *Cape Trafalgar*, in one of His Majes-
ties Frigots: from the *Cape* to *Tangier* (the wind blow-
ing fresh from the Land) a most odiferous smell, like to
Fume of Cedar or Juniper, entertain'd us; which I con-
ceive to be a mixture of pleasant scents arising from the
variety of sweet Trees and Herbs growing there wild: the
Coast rocky, rugged, and full of Hills, yet very safe for
Ships, very green with Grass and Herbs, and full of Trees.
When we came into the Bay of *Tangier*, there fell a most
vehement storm of rain, which continued an hour. . . .
Being saluted with a thousand shots of great Guns from
the Mole, the Castle, the Forts, and the Ships riding in
the Bay; we landed where we were met by the Mayor and
Corporation in their Gowns, and conducted through a
Guard of Souldiers from thence to the Castle.

The City of *Tangier* is situated very pleasantly about
the middle way between the Entrance and Mouth of the
Streights, in a large Bay like a Semi-Circle, in plain sight
of the Coast of *Spain*, being less than six Leagues distant
from it; the weather naturally very hot and scalding but
so temper'd with Friscoes and Breezes both from Land

and Sea the Air is rendered very tolerable; the Sky always bright and serene, no Rain (nor hardly any Cloud) being seen there for three parts of the year. . . .

The Castle standeth, on a Declivity, but yet insensible, of an irregular square, and fenced with a high, thin, old-fashioned Wall, having only two Gates, one towards the Country, called Porta Catharina, a wonderful strong and well-contrived Entrance; the other to the Sea, called the Water-Gate. The Streets are extreamly narrow (which is absolutely necessary in all places where the Sun is so much Vertical), which makes the Town seem much smaller, and less considerable than it is: but were they extended at the rate of the new Streets in and about London, it would take up a great deal of Ground and appear a very large Town. The Houses are low, and generally little, with Span-ish Roofs, almost flat, (which is the cause that it makes the less shew), the Walls generally of Stone and Mudd, the covering crooked Tiles, the Inside and Ceilings of Slit Deal, or Pine: There are many of the Officers and principal Townsmen, who have fine, large, commodious and well-furnished Houses and Gardens; and indeed the

Houses are for the most part very pretty and convenient. Hardly any without a little Garden, but extreamly beautiful and delighting, full of sweet Herbs and pleasant Trees, especially Vines, which running up upon Pillars made of Stone, and Espaliers made of great Reeds. . . . All their Walks and Back-sides, and Spare-places are covered and shaded with Vines. Mightily loaden with excellent Grapes of diverse sorts, sizes and shapes, and some very early ripe.

Blowing up the Harbor Mole, 1683
Samuel Pepys

Long after the period of his famous diary, Pepys kept a rather dry journal of his only visit to Tangier, in 1683, and wrote a number of letters. He was there to supervise the demolition of the great harbor mole—a strategic asset that the English had no intention of leaving to the Moors. He didn't greatly like Tangier.

Monday [17 August 1683] . . . . On shore with my Lord the first time, all the ships and the town firing guns. Met, and conducted in great state to the Castle. After dinner, see the ladies, mightily changed. The place an ordinary place, overseen by the Moors. Amazed to think how the King hath lain out all this money upon it. Good grapes and pomegranates from Spain. To-night, infinitely bit with chinchees. . . .

Sunday [14 October]. . . . Evening. On the shore till late, walking by moonshine on the Mole with Mr. Sheres. Here I had the pleasure to see in the night the volleys of great and small shot towards the sea, being the Duke of York's birth-day, and it was very pretty. . . .

Monday [15 October]. . . . Walk by moonshine in the fields under the wall, thinking of our affairs: a glow-worm shining; very small compared with what we have in England. Stayed till the gates were to be locked, and first observed the manner of placing turn pikes without the gates, for fear of horse surprising in the night. . . .

Monday [22 October]. . . . Having set them on shore at the Mole, I went in the boat round the bay. Saw very plainly the ruins of old Tangier, and the river of Tangier; Moors gathering drift-wood. Saw the manner of their huts near the water-side. To Malabar Point: . . . Coming back on the water, I first see how blue the remote hills will look about the sun's going down, as I have seen them painted, but never believed them natural.

Wednesday [24 October]. . . . Notice brought us, at dinner, of Mr. Sheres's mine to be blown up; so, some to the top of the house to see it; but I down to the water-gate, and see it blow up. The stones flew to a wonderful distance, endangering all the small vessels in the harbour. Going down to the Mole, I see the effects of the blow, which were very great, some parcels of the iron cylinder making their way quite through the side of the Mole, and, in one place, a crack from side to side across the Mole; yet of powder there was not full a barrel and a half.

Thence, I took my man, Anthony, with my long glass, and therewith entertained myself in the fields, the first time, it being a fine evening. See the whole camp of the Moors, their huts, and manner of walking up and down in their alhagues. They look almost like ghosts, all in white. As it grew dark, I went home, and there, by the gate, met with letters just come from Cadiz. . . .

Thursday [25 October]. My cold still upon me. First, took a walk on the walls, about the Irish battery; led thither to see the mortar-pieces drawn up, and placed to annoy the Moors, should they come, which my Lord does now and then think, and the more for that none of them have lately been with us, as they used to be daily. But I see nothing like extraordinary that they are doing in the fields near us.

Sailing into Tangier, 1803
Ali Bey al-Abbassi

Just over a century later, Ali Bey al-Abbassi had his first sight of Tangier, illustrating well the culture shock that it represented, as the first sight of the non-European 'East,' although since he was traveling as a Muslim, Ali should perhaps have been less surprised.

I embarked at Tarifa on board a very small vessel, and after crossing the Streights of Gibraltar in four hours, I arrived at the port of Tanja or Tangier at 10 o'clock in the morning, on the 23rd of June [1803].

The sensation which we experience on making this short passage for the first time, can be compared only to the effect of a dream. Passing in so short an interval of time, to world absolutely new, and which has not the smallest resemblance to that which we have quitted, we seem to have been actually transported into another planet.

In all countries of the world, the inhabitants of the neighbouring states are more or less united by mutual relation; they amalgamate in some degree together, and intermix so much in language, habits and customs that we pass from one to the other by gradations almost imperceptible. But this constant law of nature does not prevail between the inhabitants of the two shores of the Streights of Gibraltar; they, notwithstanding their vicinity, are as much strangers to each other as a Frenchman to a Chinese.

Close-up Squalor and Decayed Fortifications, 1816
Ali Bey al-Abbassi

The city of Tangier, viewed from the sea-side, presents a pretty regular aspect. Its amphitheatrical situation, its whitened houses; those of the Consuls, which are regularly built; the walls surrounding the town; the alcassaba, or the castle, built on a hill; and the bay, which is sufficiently spacious, and surrounded by hills, compose an interesting view; but as soon as we approach the inside of the town the illusion ceases, and we find ourselves surrounded by every thing that characterizes the most disgusting wretchedness.

Except the principal street, which is rather large, and which from the gate on the sea crosses the town in an irregular manner from east to west, all the other streets are so crooked and narrow, that scarcely three persons can pass long them in a line. The houses are so low, that one may reach the tops of most of them with the hand. The roofs are all flat, and covered with plaster. Few of the houses have high tops. The dwellings of the Consuls have decent windows; but in those of the inhabitants we see only a few, not above a foot square in size, or some loop holes, an inch or two in width, and a foot high. In some parts the principal street is badly paved; the rest is abandoned to simple nature, with enormous rocks, which they have not even taken the pains to smooth.

The walls which surround the town are in a state of total decay. They have both round and square towers; and on the land-side they are surrounded by a large ditch, which is also in ruins. Trees are planted on its sides; and it is bordered with kitchen gardens.

Adventures of a Mischievous Dog, 1921
Walter Harris

The ubiquitous Harris, at the end of the nineteenth century, found the town malodorous, and managed as always to inject a note of genial disdain, here through his dog, Balzac.

It is a queer little town, with steep streets and no cabs or carriages, very dirty and very smelly, in fact thoroughly Moresque. From the Marsa, or harbour, runs a long, straight street which ends at Bab al Sok, or gate of the market place, at the upper part of the town. In this street all the principal buildings of Tangier are situated. Here we find the large mosque—there are several in Tangier, but none of such importance as this—with its tiled minaret and prettily-carved doorway. No sight however of its interior can be obtained, for the fanatical Moors have erected a hideous green wooden screen to prevent the Christians looking in as they pass by. Contrary to Turkey and Egypt, one cannot enter the mosques in any part of Morocco, the penalty being probably a very severe thrashing from the Moors. . . . My poodle, Balzac, hearing the gurgling water of the fountain within, would put all his religious prejudices to one side and enter the sacred precincts, catching me up by leaving the building by the main gate, which I had to pass a minute or two later. What cursings used to issue from the mosque as they drove him out. . . .

But it is the people more than the buildings that form the interest of Tangier. From all over Morocco they come. The Genouah, from Timbuctoo, with their head-dresses of shells and strings and their clanking cymbals. The Susi in dark blue linen, or black and brown jelabas, the mountaineers tall and fair, many with bright blue eyes, and by far the handsomest of the Moorish peoples. The men from the Gharb, or fertile plains, enveloped in the numerous folds of their coarse haiks, speaking with a strange accent, the Berbers, with their guttural tongue absolutely different from Arabic. These are the original inhabitants of Morocco, and were Christians once. Amongst all this medley pass and repass the rich town Moors on horse or mule, gaudily caparisoned, or perhaps one may catch a glimpse of His Highness Sidi Hadj Alsalam, the Shereef of Wazan, as he rides on a splendid grey horse through the Soko, apparently indifferent to the crowd of his devout followers, who kiss the hem of his garment as he passes, and so crowd round him as to render it necessary for his slaves to beat a way for him. . . .

In winter the Soko is a vast expanse of mud, in the summer burnt clay. Here all the native traffic of Tangier is carried on. On the right lie the camels, glad of their release, no doubt, from the heavy burdens they have borne from the far-away. On the left are circles of men and boys listening to the story-tellers, watching jugglers or perhaps a performing ape, and gazing in admiration at the oft-repeated and poor performance of a snake-charmer. A little lower down are the women from the villages round selling "rhibieh," green food for horses, thistles for the mules and donkeys, chickens, eggs and bread. At the top of the Soko is a little shed, on the walls of which hang coloured waistcoats and kuftans, to tempt the young mountaineers, by their gaudy colours, to buy for their wives or daughters. Such is the scene in the Soko on a Sunday or Thursday morning.

The Politics of Water, 1901
Budgett Meakin

Tangier is drained by a primitive system of rough stone channels, which formerly opened here and there, no drains being trapped, but lately they have been entirely closed in, and have become more dangerous. The water-supply, though good, is meagre in quantity, and agitation has for many years been rife to obtain European water-works; but success has here again been frustrated by international jealousy, each power being anxious to secure the contract for a subject of its own. At present the water is brought in by two ancient conduits from wells on the Marshan and beside the Fez road.

The Jews of Tangier, 1901
Budgett Meakin

Most of the trade of Tangier, both wholesale and retail, is in the hands of the Jews, who here enjoy a liberty, and privileges utterly unknown inland; they also control the local banking. Their number can hardly be less than ten or twelve thousand, or a third of the whole population, and among the natives they are certainly the most progressive and enlightened. At their head is a Grand Rabbi, who is entrusted with judicial functions in disputes among his people. Their eleven synagogues are well attended, and the schools of the Alliance Israélite for boys and girls are well attended. These are potent factors in their social rise and growing welfare. Many Jews are employed by foreign governments in official capacities, but their places are being gradually filled by Europeans, and the attention of the Jews is turning to manufactures as well as trade. The poorer classes among them furnish most of the local craftsmen and female domestics; very few of the men do menial work, except as porters or scavengers.

The Parlous State of Tangier's Defenses, 1889
H.M.P. de la Martinière

The supervision of the batteries and carefully built works near the Kasbah is entrusted by the Sherifian government to a Spanish engineer who is attired on the occasion of grand ceremonies in a splendid uniform, glittering with gold. Three of the batteries are composed of twenty-ton

Armstrong guns, which would offer serious resistance if there existed some corps of artillery well instructed in working and firing the guns, or even in keeping them in proper order. The existence of such a corps seems doubtful when you behold the steel monsters sleeping with true Morisco nonchalance under a thick layer of dust.

Tea with the Sultan, 1816
Ali Bey al-Abbassi

Wherever the sultan was, a call on him was a mandatory high point for travelers of any distinction. Ali Bey first met Sultan Mohammed IV at Tangier and found himself warmly and almost informally treated.

The Sultan came out [of the mosque] soon after, and mounted his mule; when he came to the centre of the circle, the Kaïd and myself advanced a few steps; the Sultan stopped his mule. The Kaïd presented me; I made an inclination with my head towards him, putting my hand on my breast. The Sultan answered by a similar inclination, and said "You are welcome;" then, turning his head towards the crowd, he invited them to salute me; "Tell him," he said, "that he is welcome;" and instantly all the crowd exclaimed "welcome." . . .

The next day I went to the castle at the appointed hour. The Sultan was waiting for me on the same place with his principal Fakih or Mufti, and another favourite. He was served with tea.

When I came into his presence, he bid me ascend the small stairs and sit down by his side. He took the tea-pot and poured some tea into a cup, and having filled it up with milk, he himself presented it to me. . . .

The tea-things consisted of a gold sugar-box, a tea-pot, a milk-pot, and three cups of white china, gilt; they were all placed on a gilt dish. The sugar was put in the tea-pot, according to the custom of the country, a method not very convenient, as it compels you most frequently to take it either too much or too little sweetened.

Bad News and Clockwork Toys, 1921
Walter Harris

Harris found himself the occasional bearer of unwelcome news, particularly financial, from the French Protectorate authorities to the deposed Moulai Hafid, in exile in Tangier.

There was a room in a hideous villa that Mulai Hafid had bought as it stood, and greatly admired, that seemed haunted by the microbe of irritability. Not only was its decoration appalling, but it was full of a host of objects which the ex-Sultan had brought from Fez, amongst them innumerable musical boxes, clocks of every shape and form—he evidently particularly fancied a kind made in the shape of a locomotive engine, in coloured metals, the wheels of which all turned round at the hours, half-hours and quarters, and mechanical toys. Everything, or nearly everything, was broken, and an Italian watchmaker was employed in trying to sort out the wheels, bells and other internal arrangements of this damaged collection of rubbish. It was in this room that he had set up his workshop, and nothing pleased Mulai Hafid more than to sit and watch him.

Now it was not unseldom the writer's duty to break to the ex-Sultan the news that the French authorities refused to pay such and such a debt. With all oriental autocrats it is best to break bad news gently . . . . Just as the moment arrived to bring generalities into line with actual facts, the Italian watchmaker would meet with an unexpected success. Clocks would begin to strike and chime, or a musical-box, old and wheezy, to play, or an almost feath-erless stuffed canary in a cage would utter piercing notes in a voice that moth and rust had terribly corrupted— or from near the Italian's chair some groaning mechani-cal toy would crawl its unnatural course over the carpet, eventually to turn over on its back and apparently expire in a whizz of unoiled wheels. The ex-Sultan's attention would stray. There was an end of business. . . .

Perhaps the most difficult claim to settle was that of the Sultan's Spanish dentist, for not only was it extremely complicated, but it also became almost international. It might naturally be supposed that the dentist's bill was for professional services; but no—it was for a live lion. . . .

Now there is no possible reason in the world why dentists should not be employed to buy lions. It is not, of course, usual, and so sounds incongruous. In Morocco views as to the limitations of professions are much less restricted than with us. In Mulai Abdul Aziz's time, a very few years ago, one of the duties of the Scotch Court-piper was to feed the kangaroos, the professional photographer made scones, a high military authority supplied the Sultan's ladies with under-linen, and the gardener from Kew was entrusted with the very difficult task of teaching macaw parrots to swear. And so it was not surprising that the dentist became a buyer of lions.

The Writers

ALI BEY AL-ABBASSI (Domingo Badia y Leblich, 1767–1818), who visited Morocco between 1803 and 1805, was an enigmatic man, a Spaniard from Barcelona who was explorer and spy in the Islamic world. Claiming to be a descendant of the Abbasid caliphs, he traveled and behaved in every way as a Muslim, but when he died in Damascus in 1818 he was denied Muslim burial because a cross was found on his person.

ELLIS ASHMEAD-BARTLETT (1888–1931) was a war correspondent, who reported from Morocco for Reuters in 1907–08, 'embedded,' as we would say today, with the

French army. He covered many other wars but is most famous for his highly critical coverage of the Gallipoli campaign.

19, 68   **STEPHEN BONSAL** (1865–1951) was an American war correspondent for the *New York Herald* and the *New York Times* and a senior officer in the American Expeditionary Force in the Great War. He acted as Woodrow Wilson's personal translator at the Paris Peace Conference, served as a US diplomat in Peking, Seoul, Tokyo, and Madrid in the 1890s, and won the Pulitzer Prize for history in 1945.

10   **PAUL BOWLES** (1910–99) was an American novelist, composer, musician, poet, and translator who lived for forty-four years between Tangier and Ceylon, becoming a symbol of the louche but creative foreign community of Tangier and, more importantly, an eloquent voice in explaining and celebrating Moroccan culture through novels, music, and short stories.

TITUS BURCKHARDT (1908–84) was a Swiss connoisseur of Islamic art, writer on Islam, publisher of Sufi texts, and a devotee of the Perennial Philosophy in its 'Traditionalist' form, drawing heavily on Islamic mysticism.

ROBERT CUNNINGHAME GRAHAM (1852–1936) was a Scottish adventurer and politician. Having worked as a gaucho and fencing-master in Argentina, he traveled in Morocco in the 1890s and later became a socialist MP and the first president of the Scottish National Party.

WALTER HARRIS (1866–1933) was the *Times* correspondent in Morocco from 1887, a wealthy Englishman who spent much of his life in the country, daringly traveling in disguise in the interior, befriending sultans and rebels, and writing several books on the country and its politics, in which he was deeply involved.

EMILY KEENE, Shareefa of Ouazzane (c.1850–1941) was an English governess in Tangier who was swept off her feet and married in 1873 by the Grand Sheikh of Ouazzane, Hadj Ahmed ben Abdesslam, Morocco's leading hereditary saint and a notable dipsomaniac. After his death in 1892, she remained in Tangier until her own death in her early nineties.

DR WILLIAM LEMPRIÈRE (1739–1834) was an adventurous military surgeon, who volunteered in 1787, while serving in Gibraltar, to answer a call to treat the sultan's son, and was only allowed to leave Morocco two years later. His resulting book was a much-reprinted success. Lemprière retired from the army as Inspector-General of Hospitals.

(PERCY) WYNDHAM LEWIS (1882–1957), was an English painter and writer who visited Morocco in 1931 to escape the furor in London over the publication of his sympathetic book about Adolf Hitler. His *Filibusters in Barbary* was later republished with a manuscript called *Souks and Kasbahs* under the new title *Journey into Barbary*.

WILLIAM LITHGOW (1582–1645) was a Scot from Lanarkshire who spent many years traveling in Scotland, the

Low Countries, France, and the Empire before setting off in 1609 for Rome and thence Greece, the Middle East, and Egypt. He followed this with journeys through North Africa, Spain, and central Europe. His great book *The Totall Discourse . . .* was first published in 1632.

Pierre Loti (Louis Marie-Julien Viaud, 1850–1923) was a French naval officer and novelist. He accompanied a diplomatic mission to Fes in the late 1880s, and wrote copiously on exotic, often non-European subjects, to great contemporary acclaim. He was elected to the Academie Française in 1881.

H.M.P. de la Martinière (1859–1923)—delightfully, the 'P' is for Poisson—was a French diplomat and archaeologist who served, with a short break in Algiers, at the French Legation in Tangier from 1882 to 1901. He traveled in southern Morocco and led excavations at Volubilis and Lixus.

121 **André Maurois** (1885–1967) was a French writer, with a large output of novels, biographies, and other works. He acted as liaison officer with British forces in the First World War and as Official Observer at British HQ in the Second. His books often treat British subjects. He was elected to the Academie Française in 1938.

55 **Gavin Maxwell** (1914–69) was a Scottish naturalist, famous for his work with, and writing about, otters, and for his journey with Wilfred Thesiger through the marshes of southern Iraq, which became his book *A Reed Shaken by the Wind*. In 1966 he traveled in Morocco and published the entrancing and indispensable *Lords of the Atlas*.

21, 23, **Budgett Meakin** (1866–1906) was the editor of *The*
30, 32, *Times of Morocco*, the country's first newspaper, founded
39, 41, by his father at Tangier in 1884. He wrote extensively
136 about Morocco, including an Arabic dictionary, and after leaving in 1895, spent the rest of his life in Hampstead, writing.

Louis-Charles-Emile Mercier (1879–1945) was French vice-consul in Rabat soon after the turn of the twentieth century, and wrote several books on language and culture. His *Topographic Description of Rabat* (1906) is an indispensable account of the city just before the French Protectorate.

Charles Alfred Payton (1843–1926) was British consul in Mogador from 1880 until 1895, having already lived there in a private capacity. In 1890 his consular remit was expanded to cover the whole of southern Morocco. An easy-going man and fanatical angler, he combined his diplomatic duties with acting as angling correspondent for *The Field* from 1867 to 1914.

Samuel Pepys (1633–1703) the diarist was a member of the Privy Council's Tangier Committee since 1661, he was brought out of retirement to supervise the demolition of the harbor mole in 1684, and kept a second diary during his visit.

123   **GEORGE PHILIPS** (c.1599–1696) was secretary to the governor of Tangier, William O'Brien, Earl of Inchiquin. He arrived with his patron at Tangier in 1675, and was soon sent home to plead Inchiquin's case to the Commissioners for Tangier, after a disastrous cattle-raid in which 134 British soldiers were killed by the Moors. His letter to the lord chancellor of Ireland, a relative of Inchiquin's, was a part of the same campaign of justification.

38   **SAMUEL PURCHAS** (c.1577–1626) was a parish priest and not a traveler (he claimed never to have gone more than two hundred miles from his birthplace at Thaxted, Essex), but a compiler, editor, and rewriter of the accounts of others. He interrogated seaman and merchants, taking down their stories, and inherited a huge collection of manuscripts from Richard Hakluyt. Of these sources he made his great books of travels.

22, 65   **JAMES RICHARDSON** (1809–51) was an English explorer and anti-slavery campaigner who first traveled to Ghat and Ghadames in the Sahara in 1845. He did so again in

1850, crossing the Hammada plateau, the first European to make the crossing. He died at Bornu in 1851.

FRANÇOIS PIDOU DE SAINT OLON (1640–1720) was a French diplomat who was sent to Morocco in 1693 by Louis XIV. His three-week mission, which was unsuccessful, was to negotiate and sign a treaty; and to secure the release of French prisoners by means of an exchange for Moroccans in France.

89, 91

NICHOLAS SHAKESPEARE (1957–) is a British novelist, short story-writer, and biographer of spectacular range and virtuosity. Among many more important works, he wrote in 1999 for the *Telegraph* an account, called "Journey to the End of the World," of a visit to Mogador (Essaouira), which remains high on the list of classic writing about Morocco.

80

GABRIEL VEYRE (1871–1936) was originally a pharmacist, who traveled the world promoting the Lumière Brothers' new cinema technology, until in 1901 he was hired by Sultan Abdel Aziz as photography teacher. He fulfilled

50, 72, 74

this and a good many other roles until 1905. He then settled in Casablanca, where he spent the rest of his life in restless technological innovation, importing Morocco's first motor car and establishing its first radio station, breeding ostriches and making ice, and farming asphodels to extract fuel from them.

4, 104, 106 **EDITH WHARTON** (1862–1937) was an American writer who won the Pulitzer Prize for *The Age of Innocence* and published thirty-eight books in her lifetime. She was a devotee of France, of French imperialism (in her own words, "a rabid imperialist"), and of Maréchal Lyautey, whose work in Morocco, especially in relation to Moroccan culture, she admired greatly.

94 **JOHN WINDUS** (dates unknown) accompanied the British envoy Commodore Charles Stewart on his mission to Ceuta and Meknes in 1721, negotiating and then ratifying with Moulay Ismail a commercial treaty. His book *A Journey to Mequinez* (1725) was only the second book on Morocco published in English, and enjoyed great success.

Bibliography

Al-Abbassi, Ali Bey, *Travels of Ali Bey in Morocco, Tripoli, Cyprus, Egypt, Arabia, Syria, and Turkey between the years 1803 and 1807*, London, Longman, Hurst, Rees, Orme, and Brown, 1816.

Ashmead-Bartlett, Ellis, *The Passing of the Shereefian Empire*, Edinburgh and London, W. Blackwood & Sons, 1910.

Bonsal, Stephen, *Morocco as it is, with an Account of Sir Charles Euan Smith's Recent Mission to Fez*, London, W.H. Allen, 1894.

Bowles, Paul, *The Spider's House*, London, Macdonald & Co., 1957.

Burckhardt, Titus, *Fes, City of Islam*, Cambridge, The Islamic Texts Society, 1992.

Cunninghame Graham, Robert, *Mogreb-el-Acksa: A Journey in Morocco,* London, W. Heinemann, 1898.

Harris, Walter, *The Land of an African Sultan: Travels in Morocco, 1887, 1888, and 1889*, London, Sampson Lowe, Marston, Searle, & Rivington, 1889.

Harris, Walter, *Morocco That Was*, Edinburgh and London, W. Blackwood and Sons, 1921.

Keene, Emily, Shareefa of Wazan, *My Life Story,* London, Edward Arnold, 1912.

Lemprière, William, *A tour from Gibraltar to Tangier, Sallee, Mogodore, Santa Cruz, and Tarudant: and thence over Mount Atlas to Morocco; including a particular account of the royal harem, &c.* London, J. Walter; and sold by J. Johnson; and J. Sewell, 1793.

Lewis, Wyndham, *Filibusters in Barbary,* New York, McBride, 1932.

Lithgow, William, *The Totall Discourse, Of the Rare Adventures, and painefull Peregrinations of long nineteene Yeares Travayles, from Scotland, to the most Famous Kingdomes in Europe, Asia, and Affrica,* London, Nicholas Okes, 1632.

Loti, Pierre, *Au Maroc,* Paris, Calmann Lévy, 1890.

de la Martinière, H.M.P., *Morocco: Journeys in the Kingdom of Fez and to the Court of Mulai Hassan,* London, Whittaker & Co., 1889.

Maurois, André, *Maréchal Lyautey,* London, The Bodley Head, 1931.

Maxwell, Gavin, *Lords of the Atlas: The Rise and fall of the House of Glaoua, 1893–1956,* London, Longmans, 1966.

Meakin, Budgett, *Life in Morocco and Glimpses Beyond,* London, Chatto & Windus, 1905.

Meakin, Budgett, *The Land of the Moors: A Comprehensive Description,* London, Swan Sonnenschein & Co., 1902.

Mercier, Louis, *Rabat: Description Topographique,* Archives Marocaines, volume VII, 1906.

Naval Intelligence Division, *Morocco: A Geographical Handbook,* two vols, 1941 and 1942.

Payton, Charles Alfred, *Moss from a Rolling Stone; or, Moorish Wanderings and Rambling Reminiscences,* London, The Field, 1879.

Pepys, Samuel, *The Life, Journals, and Correspondence of Samuel Pepys . . . including a Narrative of His Voyage to Tangier,* London, R. Bentley, 1841.

Philips, George, *The Present State of Tangier, in a Letter to His Grace, the Lord Chancellor of Ireland*, London, Henry Herringman, 1680

Pidou de Saint-Olon, François, *Estat présent de l'empire de Maroc*, Paris, 1694.

Purchas, Samuel, *Purchas his Pilgrimage, or Relations of the World and the Religions Observed in all Ages and places Discovered, from the Creation unto this Present*, London, printed by William Stansby for Henrie Fetherstone, 1613

Richardson, James, *Travels in Morocco,* London, Charles J. Skeet, 1860.

Shakespeare, Nicholas, "Journey to the End of the World," *Telegraph* Magazine, 26 October 1993.

Veyre, Gabriel, *Au Maroc: dans l'intimité du sultan,* Paris, Librairie Universelle, 1905.

Wharton, Edith, *In Morocco,* New York, C. Scribner's Sons, 1920.

Windus, John, *A Journey to Mequinez; the Residence of the Present Emperor of Fez and Morocco, on the Occasion of Commodore Stewart's Embassy thither for the Redemption of the British Captives in the Year 1721*, London, Jacob Tonson, 1725.

Illustration Sources

The illustrations on pages 1, 10, 46, 53, 66, 83, 103, 113, 122, 135 are from Budgett Meakin, *The Moorish Empire* (1899) and *The Moors* (1902), courtesy of the Rare Books and Special Collections Library of the American University in Cairo; 62 from an old postcard; 79 from an anonymous 18th-century French source (Wikimedia Commons); 88 from Philip Durham Trotter, *Our Mission to the Court of Marocco in 1880, under Sir J. D. Hay* (Wikimedia Commons).